within the laws of supply and demand and they are cute enough to spot a bargain that the luckless seller doesn't know he is offering!

Colleague Gerry Hughes, Features Editor of Angler's Mail, has been dabbling in old fishing books as a hobby for most of the post-war years. His collection runs into hundreds of volumes and he thinks nothing of paying £30 for a book that, he now knows will fetch £140 in the right place at the right time. Some of his experiences are related in his special book-collecting article on pages 80–82 in this Annual.

Like most collectors, Gerry and his fellow-enthusiasts have a language of their own and their hobby of buying and selling operates within a small, elite circle of book-lovers trading through shops and postal sales.

But books are just one aspect of collecting that is attracting anglers. Even a brief study of "Swap Shop" columns in the weekly issues of Angler's Mail gives good clues to the demand building up for old centre-pin reels or hand-made, built-cane rods long since displaced by mass-produced synthetics, and so on.

This edition of the Annual also features an unusual article, and some colour photographs, of Victorian and Edwardian picture postcards which used fishing, or anglers, as the butt of their jokes.

My selection was made from a comprehensive portfolio built up by a lady called Sylvia Marie Haynes, who hopes to open a Museum of Cards. By coincidence (that's being honest, as I don't claim to be clairvoyant), my decision to purchase the rights to reproduce Mrs Haynes' cards was followed by magazine articles, radio programmes and TV references to the big business developing in the collection of old picture postcards!

My intention, as always, was to interest and entertain our readers, but I may have accidentally started something where collectors of "things angling" are concerned. So turn out the loft or attic—there may be pound notes under the dust!

Whatever their future value, I hope you will enjoy the wide range of illustrated features and other items assembled in the last twelve months for this edition of ANGLER'S MAIL ANNUAL.

Editing the Annual requires a different approach to editing the weekly Angler's Mail, in the sense that we know large numbers of the Annual are purchased for newcomers to fishing—with the purchase often made by non-anglers who are apprehensive about buying a specialist fishing book but seek, instead, an interesting mixture

that is well-produced and sold at a reasonable price.

That is why you will find, within its 96 pages, a blend of articles and features specially-written for this edition and some which are selected from the files of Angler's Mail in recognition of their value in more permanent form.

My thanks to readers for their letters and to my colleagues and contributors for their help in putting this edition together. If you are new to fishing, we would like to welcome you to the "regulars" who meet us every week in Angler's Mail. A word to your newsagent will ensure that a copy is put aside. If in any difficulty, please drop me a line at Angler's Mail. King's Reach Tower, Stamford Street. London, SE1 9LS.

**JOHN INGHAM Editor**

# contents

BEACHCASTING with JOHN HOLDEN .... 4
AVON VALLEY HOLIDAYS ................... 8
by Gerry Hughes
THE ONES THAT GOT AWAY Your own
    experiences ....................................... 12
SPORTING SASKATCHEWAN .............. 15
by John Ingham
WHITHER COARSE FISHING? .............. 16
by Fred J. Taylor
HOW TO CATCH THOSE COARSE FISH .. 20
Strip drawings by Tony Whieldon
IT PAYS TO BE A 'PEEPING TOM' ......... 24
by John Bailey
THE OTHER RAY MUMFORD ................ 24
by Melvyn Russ
HOLIDAYS AFLOAT .......................... 29
by Harry Arnold
FISHING IN FULL COLOUR.............. 33–40
TACKLING UP FOR SEA FISH .............. 41
Peter Grundel's tips
RESERVOIR TROUT FISHING .............. 47
Dick Shrives helps spot the hotspots
BRITAIN'S RECORD FISH ................... 49
Full official lists
KEEPING AN EYE ON TENCH............... 54
by Barrie Rickards
FISHING IN FULL COLOUR............. 57–64

TACKLE TIPS Lift Method . . . Link Legers
    . . . Arlesey Bomb Rigs ...................... 65
SPOT THE DIFFERENCE! Chub/Dace . . .
    Rudd/Roach . . . Pollack/Coalfish ........ 68
THE SHAD MYSTERY .......................... 70
by Ron Felton
NATIONAL ANGLING CHAMPIONSHIPS
    NFA Divisional Championships, NFA
    Ladies National Championships,
    National Junior Championships, East
    Anglian Knockout Cup, Angler's Mail
    Matchman of the Year Awards ............. 72
WHERE DO YOU LOOK FOR BIG
    BREAM? ....................................... 78
by Peter Stone
IT'S ON THE SHELF Collecting old fishing
    books ............................................. 80
by Gerry Hughes
IT'S ON THE CARDS Collecting old
    picture postcards ............................. 82
by Sylvia Marie Haynes
WINTER CHUB LIKE A LIVEBAIT ........... 84
by John Wilson
ARE YOU LICENSED? Full list of Water
    [Authorities] which issue rod licences ...... 86
    [...] [Wil]liams ......... 87

£1.70

# BEACHCASTI

1) The cast begins with the sinker and terminal rig suspended from the rod tip at a distance of around four feet. The exact length of drop varies from rod to rod, and with the individual caster's power and physique; experiment to find the correct formula. The stance is adjusted so that the feet are roughly parallel to the direction of the cast.

**Y**OU can almost learn to cast from books and articles—almost but not quite. Stringing together tackle, correct stance and so on are easy enough to pick up, but what you cannot learn is that vital co-ordinating ingredient which binds tackle and technique to each other. It is an abstract quantity, a subconscious rhythm where rod and caster move in harmony. Nobody can teach it but most people can learn by experience. When it comes—and it will be sudden—you'll probably wonder why casting ever seemed difficult.

I wish there was a formula for learning to cast but there does not seem to be one yet. All I can suggest is reading as much as possible and watching proficient casters at work. Look, analyse, and ask questions. Nobody minds being asked for advice—most will be flattered to help. So if you cannot cast and the fellow next to you on the beach is whacking out 150 yards, ask him how he does it. Even if he can't tell you much, just watching him will provide food for thought.

The short cut to success is having someone on hand to pinpoint and correct your faults as you go along. Unfortunately, many beginners have to go it alone. So bearing that in mind I think it might be better to concentrate on what NOT to do rather than go through a complex description of casting styles.

As I am involved with casting, I find myself unconsciously analysing the styles of other anglers, and I would say that out of every 100 beach anglers ten cast well: ten do not and never will have a clue; the other 80 could so easily do better but don't give themselves a chance.

2) The body weight is transferred to the right leg, the body is turned away from the sea as far as is comfortable. The rod tip is held fairly high with the left ·hand as low as is comfortable. Then the sinker is swung in a pendulum arc towards and away from the caster, so that the swing of the tackle just clears the right hand side of the rod. The cast begins when the sinker reaches the top of its inswing—towards the caster.

3) Shoulders and waist rotate fairly slowly but strongly so that the rod tip gathers up the leader and sinker from their pendulum arc. There should be very little sensation of effort at this stage of the cast. This is extremely important with big weights and fast action, powerful surf rods. The left hand begins to rise and pull the rod. The right arm is bent ready for the final punch.

On the whole, three things are wrong: (1) incorrect or imbalanced tackle; (II) a stunted, upright casting method; (III) trying to cast with the arms alone.

Let's look at problems (II) and (III). To an extent they are related in that the wrong style prevents full use of the body. Arms alone cannot power a big cast—that is a simple fact of life. Yet many anglers seem to think they will achieve a hundred yards or more like it.

Long casting demands that the rod is swung through the greatest possible arc as fast and smoothly as possible, using the whole body as a power supply. Any caster not doing this must be losing out.

The cast I use for beach fishing is shown in the photographs. It is fairly easy to master and will provide adequate distances—130 yards, or more with more bait; upwards of 160 yards with lead alone. The pictures show the basics of the cast so rather than analyse those, I'll cover a few points worth bearing in mind.

The body swivels through a semi-circle during the cast. So the position of the feet is important. Stand so that during the final part of the cast the shoulders are parallel to the sea and there is no sense of over-balance to prevent full power being applied. Now turn, keeping the feet in the same place, until rod and shoulders are facing directly away from the sea. Arms are held low and fairly straight. That is the starting position.

It is more efficient to cast a swinging lead than one hanging motionless. In the latter case, the rod has to move through a considerable arc before the line tightens and the lead moves, which is all a waste of useful rod movement. Using a four-foot drop between rod tip and lead, swing the lead pendulum fashion. At the height of the back stroke—towards the caster—the cast begins. Timing takes a bit of practice; the main thing is to allow no slackness in the line or an over-run will almost certainly follow.

Initially, power comes from the legs, shoulders and hips. Relative to the body, the arms hardly move other than to control the rod arc. Only when the shoulders swing parallel to the sea does the right arm punch smoothly forward. The left arm pulls down and contributes quite considerably to the power stroke.

Exactly when to release the line is impossible to say. It is a natural reflex for most casters—you'll find it just happens. If the cast is too high, swing the rod through a lower plane and/or release later. If too low this calls for a higher arc.

Everybody gets over-runs. You must learn to live with them and eventually they will go away. They will cost line but don't let them cost tempers!

That's really all there is to it. Casting is not a mystic art or an athletic performace. If you can throw a stone 30 yards you can cast over a hundred with no great effort. The secret is probably confidence and commonsense practice. One thing is for sure—if you cast well, whole new areas of fishing will be opened.

Think about it: around Britain there is a strip of seabed just over a hundred yards out which has never seen a hook because few anglers cast that far and boats don't often fish that close in. It might fish well—it has to be worth a try, anyway!

● *For more guidance on beach-fishing techniques turn to TACKLING UP FOR SEA FISH by Peter Grundel on page 41.*

4) Shoulders swing to lie at an angle of roughly 45 degrees to the water's edge. The right arm punches and the left pulls down towards the bottom of the ribs. The acceleration must be brisk but smooth. Try to turn the rod around an imaginary pivot set midway between the hand-grips. The emphasis of power should be up into the sky, not simply out to sea. Height is essential for good casting.

5) The sinker is released and the rod unbends and flicks the tackle into the air. Timing of the cast release is something that usually occurs subconsciously. No attempt need be made to alter this natural timing unless the cast flies too high or too low.

# AVON VALLEY HOLIDAYS

*Your guide is GERRY HUGHES*

The scenery may not be all that beautiful but the fishing certainly is. Every variety of specimen fish is caught at the Royalty Fishery, Christchurch, where day tickets are obtainable at the local tackle shop— not forgetting a Water Authority rod licence.

TAKE the A338 at Salisbury towards Bournemouth—and you're on a major holiday route to the seaside. But the same road is also an angling highway as it wends down the valley of the Hampshire Avon, one of the country's most famous coarse fishing rivers.

Critics say the Avon isn't the river it was. But that is a criticism which can now be levelled at many waters and the facts are that the Avon's strong current, clear water and strong weed growth houses many big roach, chub, barbel, pike and dace, plus grayling, trout and salmon.

The Hampshire Avon is not the jealously-guarded private preserve that many believe it to be. There are plenty of stretches available for a visitor and the surrounding countryside also offers superb stillwater fishing.

The best tip for anyone contemplating an Avon Valley holiday is to contact the two big local clubs—Salisbury & District AC and Ringwood & District AA. Both clubs have open memberships and offer more fishing than a holiday visitor can hope to cover during the average stay.

For example, Salisbury club offers a mile of Avon fishing at Burgate, another mile at Charford, three miles

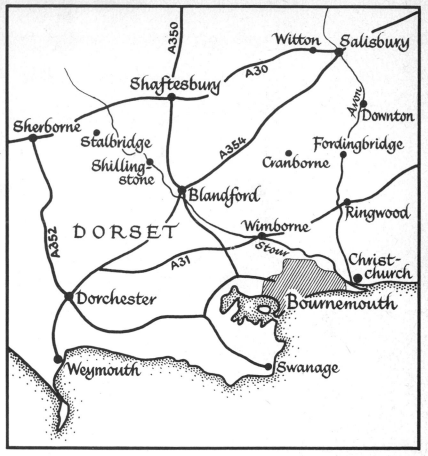

**If it's big barbel you want to fight, no need to look further than the Royalty Fishery, one of the most famous on the Hampshire Avon. This double-figure specimen was landed close to the Fishery Office.**

The Dorset Stour at Longham, a stretch of the river noted for chub. It also holds big dace and the thick weedbeds are safe refuge for plenty of rod-benders.

How about that, then? Stan Copperthwaite, the London Anglers Association bailiff at Britford, near Salisbury, puts a 9 lb. barbel on the scales. A number of 2 lb. roach have also been caught from this stretch.

at Salisbury itself, three more at Durnford, two at West Amesbury and another mile at Ratfynn Farm. The club also has two miles of the River Nadder, the same amount of the River Wylye, half-a-mile of the River Bourne and almost a mile of the famous Dorset Stour. Some stretches are reserved for trout only, but the majority are for coarse fishing.

If stillwater coarse fishing is a holiday preference, the Salisbury club controls Steeple Langford Lakes, Petersfinger Lakes, Edington Lake and Milford Lake.

**Membership forms and full details are available from the Secretary, Salisbury DAC, 28 Dudley Avenue, Fordingbridge, Hants.**

For a short visit, day tickets are sold for some of the individual waters, as follows: Steeple Langford Lakes, contact E. Briant, 6 The Wirrell, Steeple Langford, Salisbury. For Edington Lake contact G. Drewett, Priory Farm, Edington, Westbury, Lee's Store, 34, Cold Harbour Lane, Salisbury, sells tickets for the town water. Avon Angling & Sports shop sells tickets for Charford Fishery. V. Stallard, Burgate Manor Farm, Burgate, Fordingbridge, sells tickets for the Burgate length. Tickets for the Nadder at Bemerton are available from Whitneys Newsagents, 187 Wilton Road, Salisbury.

Salisbury & District AC also has an exchange ticket scheme with a number of other clubs in the area, which opens up more fishing for its members. Among the clubs concerned are Chippenham, Gillingham, Wimborne, Blandford, Bathampton, Isfield, Hastings, Billingshurst, Portsmouth, Bristol Amalgamated, Oakhanger, Christchurch, Eastleigh, Bath and Bovington.

Further downstream, Ringwood & District AA controls more good fishing. Their stillwaters include Hurst Pond, Hightown Pit and Blashford Pits, plus a stretch of the main Avon at Fordingbridge, two miles of the famous Lower Severals Fishery and nearly two miles of the equally famous Ibsley water.

The club also has a mile of trout fishing on the Moors River and stretches of the Dorset Stour at Blandford St. Mary, Stourpaine and West Parley. An exchange ticket scheme operates with Wimborne AC, Wareham AC, Sturminster & Hinton AA and the Portsmouth RN & RM fishery at Driad Lake.

**Full details are available from D. Winslade at 87 Lake Road, Verwood, Dorset.**

Membership of these two clubs

An Avon visitor deals firmly with his very first barbel while fishing between the two bridges at Ringwood, Hampshire.

alone should satisfy the most hungry of anglers—but there is more . . . London Anglers Association has two Avon stretches—one at Britford and the other at Burgate.

**You can find out more about these waters by writing to the LAA at 183 Hoe Street, Walthamstow, London, E.17, asking for details of the associate membership scheme.**

Still not enough? Then try the day-ticket stretch of the Bull Hotel at Downton—the most famous fishing pub in the Avon Valley—the three miles controlled by the Bat and Ball at Breamore, the Somerley Fishery and the Plaish House Hotel water at Winkton.

But most famous Avon stretch of all is the Royalty Fishery, Christchurch, where many huge fish have been caught. Tickets are available only from Davis Tackle Shop, Bargates, Christchurch, where the owner also sells tickets for Winkton Fishery and Christchurch AC's waters in the harbour (which produces good coarse fish plus saltwater species such as mullet and flounders) and the lower Dorset Stour.

The Dorset Stour offers the chance of big fish including barbel, chub, pike dace and roach. The best-known of its ticket waters is Throop Fishery, some six miles of river at Holdenhurst, just

outside Christchurch. Tickets from the bailiff at South Lodge, Holdenhurst.

There is also fishing available at Longham, where the Bridge House Hotel has a stretch of river, Corfe Mullen (tickets from the Old Mill Guest House), Canford Bridge, Wimborne (tickets from Newman's Boathouse). Conyer's Tackle Shop in West Street, Blandford Forum, issues tickets for Blandford & District AC's stretch.

The Post Office in Durweston issues tickets for the local club stretch at Blandford and the Crown Hotel, Stalbridge, does the same for Stalbridge AS water. Tickets for Sturminster & Hinton AA's seven-mile stretch can be bought from club secretary B. Redpath, 46, Rush Close, Sturminster Newton, Dorset.

Wessex Water Authority has recently opened a seven-acre coarse fishery and a trout lake of the same size at Pallington, near Dorchester. Both are available on day tickets. Don't forget other trout fisheries in the area. There are the famous Damerham Trout Lakes near Ringwood, Allens Farm at Sandleheath and Leominstead at Emery Down, near Lyndhurst.

●*Adapted and condensed from VALLEY OF THE AVON, first published in Fishing Holidays by IPC Magazines Ltd. 1975. Revised and updated by Gerry Hughes for Angler's Mail Annual 1980. ©Copyright IPC Magazines Limited.*

## A sting in the tale

IN the uninterrupted sunshine which characterised Whitsun 1974, Peter and I had been feeding the crabs contentedly for several hours, the weather more than compensating for the absence of fish. Anchored in a small boat off Bradwell, in barely five feet of water, the prospect of luring anything more than an inquisitive eel seemed utterly remote. Slack water on a neapish low tide rates a resounding yawn from all who fish the East Coast estuaries regularly and we had no reason to expect this one to be any different.

Spurred on by the prospect of poached eels for supper, I threaded two large lugworms on to my 2/0 hook and cast them a long way astern in the direction of the sewage outfall. If there were eels about, this was surely where they would congregate!

The bite, when it came, was as astonishing as the rest of the tale. There was no hint of movement in the rod tip, instead the spool on my multiplier began to rotate, slowly at first but with gathering speed in spite of the fact that I had set the star drag recklessly tight.

Seizing the rod, I struck hard and announced to Peter that I had snagged the bottom. But the "bottom" plodded off, unimpressed by my efforts to restrain it!

After 20 minutes, I had succeeded in bringing the fish to the boat, but failed on this and all subsequent attempts to lift it from the bottom—all of five feet away! I allowed the fish to take line as it set off once again for the deeper water, and decided to tire it still further in the hope that it would surface. But it didn't.

Nothing that my stiffish boat rod and 30 lb nylon leader could do would persuade that fish to leave the bottom. After 30 minutes of such antics, I was exhausted and handed my rod to Peter to let him take over and beat the monster. After 15 minutes, he returned the rod to me with a glint in his eye. "I don't want to steal your fun," he said (liar!).

For a further 10 minutes, I battled with the fish which by this time Peter had decreed to be a sting-ray of monstrous proportions (although neither of us had seen anything). After playing the "ray" for almost an hour without any hint of it tiring, Peter seized the rod back and said "I'll show you how we handle these big rays in Dorset".

He then proceeded to jam his thumb against the side of the spool in a last-ditch attempt to winch in the ray. There was a sharp crack as the line parted at the leader knot.

"I'm sorry, Pat," he said. "Very sorry . . . but you really must learn to tie better knots. I'll show you how we tie them in Dorset . . ."

A little over a week later a shore angler named Alan Perkins fishing the identical spot hooked and landed a sting-ray on bass tackle. The fish was five feet long, three feet wide and over a foot thick.

Southend angling journalist Bob Cox estimated the fish to weigh over 70 lb, but it was never actually weighed and was returned to the sea alive. If Bob is right this fish would have beaten the existing record by more than 10 lb. And if I am right, I lost a national record that day, doing things, Dorset's way!

**PATRICK LEATHEM,**
**Caversham,**
**Berks.**

# GOT AWAY...

## Soaked, breathless and fishless

SOME years ago a friend and I witnessed a "lost monster" incident which, if related by the would-be captor to strangers, might well be considered unbelievable.

We were fishing the top lake at Earlswood Common and hadn't been there long when we were disturbed by frantic, almost hysterical calls for help.

On the bottom lake a pike fisherman had hooked a huge fish which promptly rounded the diving board in the lake and then found shelter in the dense weedbeds.

The angler's first idea was that as the line had gone around the diving board, the rod and reel should follow, thus putting him once more in direct contact with the fish. Luckily, the lake was shallow at the far end and by carefully paying out line but still maintaining pressure he was able to wade out waist-deep across the lake.

His line became caught on a snag halfway and the only solution was to wade back across to free it. This accomplished, he was now back to square one. Having previously tried giving slack, and then continuous pressure, to no avail he now became desperate.

Leaving his rod securely wedged he disappeared, returning some 15 minutes later with a small inflatable dinghy. His intention was to paddle around the diving board until he had retrieved all his line and then to exert upwards pressure on the fish.

Many breathless minutes later the craft was inflated and dropped unceremoniously on to the lake. But there were concrete steps leading into the water and when the would-be captor lowered himself belly down, into the dinghy, the sharp stones penetrated the bottom. Flat on his stomach, and with the rod in one hand he was unable to do anything without risking another soaking, and once more summoned help.

I was able to lift him from the sinking dinghy but our help did not save him from a soaking as he was far too heavy for me to lift completely and my grasp slackened, letting him fall face down into the lake.

His patience was now at an end. He had spent almost £6 on the dinghy—which was now useless—suffered several hours of wet clothing and, worse still, his fags and matches could not provide comfort as they, too, were wet.

As he was preparing to pull for a break the fish moved off. But after a brief battle the line went slack and the fish was gone.

**ALAN STARLING,
Coulsdon, Surrey.**

## Chub had last laugh

IT was one of those summer evenings when you walk the dog along the local stretch of river, just browsing over the water before the weekend assault. The chub and dace seem to congregate under the over-hanging willows, soaking up the last of the sun's rays, in defiance of all anglers.

Deciding it was time to head for home, I took a last look—and that's when it started. I looked back over the gently rising dace and all hell broke loose as a chub unleashed his power and made a mighty splash.

On the following Sunday, with this memory still fresh, I decided to have a go for him. As I tackled up, I could still see the occasional chub, which would do a submarine act and disappear into the murky depths. Not discouraged, I fished most of the day just catching "tiddlers" but there was no sign of the monster chub.

As evening crept on, I decided to call it a day but as I was emptying my keepnet I remembered a new spinner I had bought some time before, which was still in its box. I had tried legered and floatfished minnow earlier without success, so I tied on this expensive spinner and cast it out. But I overcast and the spinner was flashing away in mid-air hanging from a willow opposite.

Thinking that I should perhaps have gone home earlier I managed to free it and it splashed into the water with a crash that should have scared off the fish for at least 200 yards in

either direction. Undaunted, I started to reel in the slack line and you can probably guess what happened.

That identical water-thrashing tail appeared, the spinner vanished and I struck instantly, my rod tip travelling freely through the air without taking up enough slack line to make proper contact.

It's amazing that the gears on my reel weren't fused together with the speed of my winding-in seemingly miles of line, but the big chub just spat out the spinner and vanished.

Fed up, I started to walk to the road and as I looked back to the scene there came that familiar splash, just to let me know that he was still free.

I'm sure I saw him laughing. But be warned, fish. I'll have my revenge!
**RICHARD BROOKE,**
**Cowley, Oxford.**

# Small boy's big roach

THE setting was the bird sanctuary at Evesham, a regular venue for me as a lad. In my imagination I was a soldier in the jungle as Dad and I would climb across the dam, battle through 7 ft. high "stingers" (well, they always seemed that tall!), then struggle through brambles and walk beneath the lone apple trees.

I remember that the sun always shone and we would set up quietly as the mist cleared from the water. "Now you stay here, and keep quiet!"—Dad always said that!

I would watch proudly as Dad walked precariously out along the planks to where the boat was moored. A great chasm separated us—about 15 feet.

On this particular morning I put a maggot on my No. 20 hook, tied to about 3 lb. line. This was attached to my best rod—a garden cane. Well money was scarce in those days.

I started fishing with great determination in two feet of gin-clear water, then I caught a stickleback and shouted gleefully.

"Shut up and be careful," shouted Dad.

It was then I saw it move—a giant ghost moving slowly beneath the old wooden planks. I lowered my small offering down through the planks to the waiting giant and watched in amazement as it sucked my maggot down.

As I struck, all hell broke loose.

Well, you can imagine a lad about 11 years old with a garden cane stuck down between the planks of the landing stage, screaming for his Dad to come and look.

"What the hell's going on? What have you done now? Where's this big fish then?" he asked.

"Underneath the planks, Dad," replied my meek voice.

He got down on his hands and knees and peered between the planks into the water. "My God, that's the biggest roach I've ever seen," he exclaimed.

I didn't know Dad's eyes opened that wide! Suddenly the roach, which Dad reckoned to be 2½–3 lb., took off.

I sat there, tears running from my eyes, while Dad said: "Never mind, son, there will be another time".

One thing came from that day in my childhood which I will never forget. Dad bought me a rod, reel, line and even a basket—and I'm still trying to catch that roach!
**DAVID PURNELL,**
**Northfield,**
**Birmingham.**

# Eel with a taste for trout

IT was getting dark and the bats were darting low over the small weirpools into which I had just made my last cast of the evening. The float, a minute dot of orange sliding down the current, shot to the side and stabbed under.

A sweeping strike was answered by a solid jag and another small trout came kicking towards the bank. This one, about six inches long, had swallowed the hook so I dropped it back into the water while I fumbled about for my disgorger.

While sorting through my haversack I became aware of a rustling sound and looked to see my rod moving steadily towards the pool. I took a dive to save my tackle and the rod arched round as I struck hard, but excitement gave way to annoyance as I realised I had hooked the tree roots beneath my feet.

Everything was tried to trace the hook but all in vain until I slackened off, when there was a sudden movement beneath the roots and my line streaked away. As I tightened, the rod was yanked downwards and I only just managed to release the bail arm in time to prevent a "smash".

The fish surged off around the weirpool, occasionally giving a terrific tug that sent my rod tip lunging downwards. This continued for some time until, quite suddenly, everything went slack and I felt that hopeless feeling common to all anglers at times like this.

As I wound in, I realised I was taking up yards of slack line and it suddenly dawned on me that the fish was still on, but had changed direction and moved towards me. I began to turn the handle more hastily and then one of the most amazing fishing experiences I have ever had took place.

Right beneath my feet, an ugly head and neck suddenly popped out of the water. A great black eel sat up in the pool and stared at me in disgust for a few seconds—and then I swear it spat the hook at me before slinking back into the depths.

Stunned, I watched the ripples spreading over the surface as another bat swooped past and away into the darkness.
**DAVID TIPPING,**
**North Ripon,**
**Leeds.**

# Sporting Saskatchewan

## by JOHN INGHAM

WHEN Air Canada launched a Western Arrow direct service from London Heathrow to the city of Saskatoon, in Saskatchewan, Northern Canada, I joined the inaugural flight to sample the fabulous fishing at La Ronge, 236 miles further on in the far north where the Hudson's Bay Company established a trading post in the early 1900s.

Lake La Ronge was "discovered" in 1946 when a road was constructed to a community of hunters, fishermen and trappers. Anglers were among the first to take to the new road and in growing numbers they went afloat to seek specimens in the vast lake of 500 square miles that still provides some of the best sport anywhere in the world for pickerel, Northern pike and lake trout.

The trading post is now a thriving centre with a resident population of more than 3,000 people. But the town bustles in the tourist season with a holiday invasion of Americans, Canadians and others from the four corners of the world.

From La Ronge holidaymakers can branch out to other northern adventure playgrounds, using road, 'plane or boats to reach the enchanting natural summer beauty of Saskatchewan's northern territory.

Beaches, cabins and camping grounds of English Bay, Nemeiben Lake and Waden Bay are only minutes away on Highway No. 2. Beautiful Otter Lake (Missinipe) and Otter Rapids is an hour's drive. Or a short flight reaches historic Stanley Mission on the Churchill River. There are also many drive-in and fly-in camps scattered throughout the region.

Angling visitors with a taste for history can see "petrographs", or Indian rock paintings, along the cliffs of the Churchill River. These are 2,000 and 3,000 years old—relatively youthful considering that the story of the first people of Saskatchewan began about 15,000 years ago when, at the time of the last great Ice Age, the ancestors of modern-day Indians arrived across the Bering Strait from Europe and Asia.

Ron and Eve Mackay were my hosts at Red's Camps, La Ronge, where our party of journalists and travel agency representatives were accommodated in comfortable motel-type rooms at a base camp on the lake shore.

They also run "out-camps" at Besnard, 37 air miles from La Ronge on the Churchill river system, reached by floatplane in about 20 minutes, and at Costigan, 132 miles north of La Ronge.

Our fishing trips on Lake La Ronge were restricted by unusually poor weather for mid-summer and by a travel schedule that packed in visits to other tourist centres, Provincial Government receptions and other forms of hospitality for which the Canadians are justly famous—but obviously possessed of greater stamina than us!

But we put in a full day on the lake and even non-anglers on board the Red's Camps high-powered motor boats managed a very respectable mixed bag of pickerel or walleye (pike-perch or zanders) and a few of the big lake trout that run to 30 lb. or more.

Under the watchful eye of Cree Indian guides, supplied by Ron Mackay, our baited spoons trolled at various depths and most of the party were soon in action. If there is a criticism to offer—and one not usually encountered among regular anglers!—sport was too easy and our lunch-break on one of the lake's thousand islands, quickly filled the Indians' frying pans with tasty fresh-caught pickerel

Ron Mackay and his wife have organised a well-stocked tackle shop in the base camp at La Ronge with a good selection of lures, lines, rods and reels.

They charge (1978 prices) from 23 dollars upwards per day, depending on the type of accommodation wanted and the number in the party.

A boat fitted with a 40 h.p. Johnson outboard (the fastest ride I'm ever likely to take across any fishing lake!) costs 36 dollars a day. Guides charge 35 dollars a day plus five dollars per additional boat.

*Local contact for prices/leaflets:* Ron and Eve Mackay, Red's Camps Ltd., Box 67, La Ronge, Saskatchewan, Canada SOJ 1 LO. General brochures on fishing and travel facilities in Saskatchewan are normally available from the London offices of the Provincial Government of Saskatchewan at 14–16 Cockspur Street, Trafalgar Square, London SW1Y 5BL and branches of Air Canada. Lunn-Poly and Pickfords travel agencies can probably arrange favourable terms for clubs or groups.

● *Colour photographs of fishing action on Lake La Ronge are on pages 38 and 39.*

Colour photographs of fishing action on Lake La Ronge are on pages 38 and 39.

## HOLIDAY TARGETS

NORTHERN PIKE—The most widely-distributed fish in Saskatchewan and known locally as jackfish. Try light spinning tackle, bait-casting and/or baited shallow-running lures. Average weight 2 lb.–10 lb. Saskatchewan record: 42 lb. 10 oz.

WALLEYE (*pickerel*). Found in all but the shallowest lakes. Good table fish. They take bait slowly so don't be in a hurry to strike. Average 1 lb.–3 lb. Saskatchewan record: 14 lb. 3 oz.

LAKE TROUT. The only trout native to Saskatchewan waters. Average 5 lb. but 30-pounders taken each year. Heavy trolling tackle needed or "jigging", Cree Indian style. Saskatchewan record: 51 lb. 10 oz.

ARCTIC GRAYLING. Found in the clear, fast streams of the far north. Try dry fly with dark flies or quarter-ounce light spinners. Average 1 lb.–2 lb.

Saskatchewan record: 4 lb. 5 oz.

RAINBOW TROUT. Successfully introduced to a number of Saskatchewan waters and now average 2 lb.–3 lb. Saskatchewan record: 18 lb.

BROOK TROUT. Introduced in the 1920's and now well-established. Dry or wet fly or light spinning. Averages less than 1 lb. in streams but 1 lb.–2 lb. in lakes. Saskatchewan record: 6 lb. 2 oz.

BROWN TROUT. Found in creeks and streams of Cypress Hills area. Skilled dry fly fishing will catch them. Average 2 lb. Saskatchewan record: 15½ lb.

OTHER SPECIES. Perch are widely distributed throughout Saskatchewan's lakes; whitefish in lakes/rivers; sauger in Saskatchewan River and Churchill River; goldeye and sturgeon in the Saskatchewan river and Cumberland Lake area. Splake (a cross between brown and lake trout) are being stocked in some lakes on an experimental basis.

# WHITHER COAR

Match anglers line the banks of the River Lea Relief Channel at Waltham Abbey. Are matchmen, with their sophisticated approach to fishing, driving away those who fish only for fun and pleasure? Fred J. Taylor thinks so and says the "magic" of June 16 has faded.

*After 50 years in angling, FRED J. TAYLOR has retired and emigrated with his wife to Australia to join his daughter and son-in-law. Before he left, Fred set down these hard-hitting views on modern coarse fishing and what needs to be done to help beginners and to help the sport expand again. He accuses matchmen of making fishing too difficult . . . charges specimen hunters with creating a nightmare of secrecy, ill-feeling, technical jargon and mumbo-jumbo . . . and pleads the cause of fun and pleasure anglers who, he says, are leaving the ranks.*

# SE FISHING? BY FRED J. TAYLOR

There was a time, not so many years ago, when I could have taken a young angler or a complete novice to certain stretches of a canal or river, fixed them up with a run-of-the-mill float, pinched on a couple of shot, baited a No. 12 hook with a couple of maggots, and felt confident that my companion would at least get some bites.

These days, in the same places, I would have to think in terms of a 1lb. bottom, a No. 20 hook and an incredibly sensitive, accurately shotted float before even considering the bait.

Even then the chances would be that this sophisticated and technical approach—to what should be a contemplative and relaxing sport—would be too much for a novice to handle.

In 50 years of fishing I have tried to keep upsides with modern developments and, thankfully, I still have access to waters where my fishing can be regarded as sheer relaxation and

not bloody-minded technical achievement. But these waters are few and far between and becoming fewer as matchfishing becomes more and more demanding.

I never could compete with the top matchmen. I never wanted to and I certainly would have found no pleasure in fishing if that had been the only kind available to me.

I am not competitive—all the competition I need is between me and the fish. What grieves me is that the future of coarse fishing is now no longer showing the promise it did some 20 years ago. We boast that we are members of Britain's biggest participant sport, which may well be so, but only if we take into account the thousands of sea and trout anglers.

Coarse fishing may be on the increase on the match side, though I have my doubts even in that respect. In some quarters specimen hunting has become a nightmare of secrecy,

ill-feeling, technical jargon and plain out-and-out mumbo-jumbo. And in between we have the ordinary Mr. Average angler whose ranks, whether you like it or not, are dwindling. The kids are discouraged because their fishing becomes either more difficult or less available as the seasons pass by.

Swims once packed with casual anglers—out for a few hours on their day or half-day off—are now vacant because the anglers themselves are not prepared to flog themselves to death to catch below-average fish. They do not have the technical skills of the matchman who knows how to extract every ounce of fish out of a given swim, and who, more importantly, enjoys doing it. Neither are they prepared to develop those technical skills to catch the odd fish. Theirs is a different attitude.

*Continued on next page*

Although I have never been deeply involved in matchfishing I have put in just as much effort, just as much time and developed just as many ideas in the other field. At one stage it was important to me that I should catch bigger-than-average fish. I wanted to prove myself. I was just as dedicated as any top matchman—but my approach and techniques were different.

It took me years to achieve certain goals but I achieved them out of sheer persistence. Then I realised I was no longer enjoying myself. I needed the sleep I was losing. Those Monday morning headaches were self-inflicted through lack of sleep, glaring sun and nonstop fishing.

So I tried to become an ordinary (for want of a better phrase) pleasure angler. My weekly column in Angler's Mail was for some time published under the heading "Fishing for Fun". But in recent years it has become more and more noticeable that fun and pleasure anglers are leaving our ranks. Scores of my good coarse fishing friends have taken to the sea. At least, they say, the fish are not hook-shy or bait-shy or stunted; they're not too difficult to catch and worth catching now that fish-shop prices are so high.

I could name hundreds of coarse fishing companions and club members who, at one time, used the Close Season gap as an excuse to "have a dabble" for trout. But as soon as June 16 arrived their trout rods were put away and they went back to what they called "proper fishing".

Now they don't bother. The magic of June 16 does not seem to be present any more. Thoughts of big rainbows are still in their minds and the general excitement of the "midnight countdown" just isn't what it was.

I am fortunate in that I can fish one of the best tench waters in the country and, recalling the old magic of years gone by, I decided in 1978 to practise the midnight-on-June-15 ritual as I had done so many times in seasons past. In those days we could have counted on 30 or more members dragging swims, putting boats in position, setting up bankside pitches, pre-baiting and literally watching the clock, ready to cast at midnight.

But in 1978, at Wotton Lakes, the season opened with six anglers at the water. Even the dawn invasion, which could usually be relied upon to produce another dozen or more anglers loaded with tackle and bait, did not materialise. Less than a dozen anglers shared both magnificent lakes and I marvelled at the change that had taken place.

The general fishing at Wotton has not become more difficult. The tench fishing is harder because the tench have become more nomadic in view of the shortage of weed. But the roach and rudd fishing has been incredibly good. No matches are held at Wotton, nor is it overfished, and I wonder why it is exploited so little.

Perhaps our members know it will never be overcrowded or overfished and that those who fish there are out for pleasure and not for blood. We have our experts and our big fish catchers but there are no secrets. Of course, ours is an almost unique situation and yet I hear from other clubs holding long stretches of river, and big lake complexes, that their membership drops each season.

"We rely on the pleasure angler—the once-a-week dabbler to keep our club going, but the whole administration revolves around who has won which match and who will represent us in the 'National'," the secretary of a big association told me recently.

And he went on: "I am not anti matchfishing but the sooner we begin to consider the ordinary chap who simply wants to spend an hour or two at the water without a load of rules, regulations, bans or restrictions, the sooner we are going to build up our membership. But we shall not attract Mr. Average if our matchmen keep making fishing more and more difficult. They have developed even the catching of immature roach to an exact science and, today, the ordinary angler, who aims his tackle a dozen times a year, simply finds the going too hard. That is fact, not fiction."

Those, as near as I remember, were his exact words and they bring me back to my opening remarks.

Whether we are match-minded or not, we have made our fishing too difficult for the beginner to appreciate. For years it has been regarded as a crime to kill a fish. For years we have caught and returned damaged, injured or ill-conditioned fish, and when our waters have stopped producing as many bites as we would like, we scream for them to be restocked.

We have allowed disease to wipe out stocks. We have insisted on sick fish being transferred to other waters instead of being buried as they should have been. We have refused to believe that a scientist could possibly tell us anything about fish culture, and when we've been asked to allow a few specimens to be killed for research purposes, we have refused!

No one wants fishing as easy as I have had it in such places as Northern Canada, where an absolute non-angler can catch as many as the expert, but we have been stubborn, pigheaded and miserly about the whole business.

There has been talk of fish farms that are to produce fish for barren waters and for some reason this has been regarded as real progress. Progress my foot! What we need to spend our money on is making waters clean enough to support fish. Then there will be no need to restock from fish farms. Coarse fish are just about the most prolific breeders and it only takes a few pairs to replenish a barren water.

I believe that we have the finest trout conservation policy in the world. I don't agree with all the restrictions imposed but that is a personal opinion. What concerns and convinces me is that money—real money—has been spent to provide good fishing for anyone with a fly rod and a day to spend using it. The economics haven't always worked out but they have never been too far off course.

Instead of cramming in more and more immature fish for match anglers to compete for, we should surely be trying to do something for the 60 per cent who are neither matchmen nor specimen hunters.

Instead of making tackle so delicate, baits so incredibly important, shotting and floats so sophisticated that a dust shot can make the difference between fish and no fish, we should be looking to the balance of stocks and finding out how many fish or how much poundage of fish a water can accommodate.

We should not be ruled by the match minority. We should not be afraid to listen to expert advice and, above all, we should never be afraid to kill or take away the odd fish for the table. That is our right. It must always be our right. And if we exercise it a little more we may find the ranks of coarse fishermen beginning to swell once more.

Fred J. Taylor is now living in Australia—but the chances are that he's still surrounded by fishing tackle and pondering how best to tackle the Aussie specimens!

# COARSE FISHING with Tony Whieldon

## FISHING FOR CARP

**VARIETIES**

THESE VARIETIES HAVE THE SAME FEEDING HABITS, AND CAN ALL BE CAUGHT ON THE TACKLE, AND BY THE METHODS DESCRIBED HEREAFTER.

LEATHER CARP

COMMON CARP

MIRROR CARP

**CARP** (Cyprinus carpio). LIVES IN LAKES, PONDS, CANALS, AND SOME SLOW MOVING RIVERS. FOOD CONSISTS OF MICROSCOPIC ORGANISMS, BLOODWORMS, NYMPHS, WATER SNAILS, FRESH WATER MUSSELS, WEED SHOOTS, ALGAE, DAPHNIA, etc. THE LARGEST CARP EVER CAUGHT IN BRITAIN WEIGHED 44lb. AND WAS CAPTURED BY RICHARD WALKER IN 1952 FROM REDMIRE POOL. THERE ARE, HOWEVER, BIGGER ONES JUST WAITING FOR YOU.

**TACKLE**

A CARP ROD IS A MUST IF YOU INTEND TO TANGLE WITH THESE FAST AND POWERFUL FIGHTERS.

A RELIABLE FIXED SPOOL REEL IS ALSO NEEDED, LOADED WITH ABOUT 200yds OF 10lb LINE. DON'T RISK FISHING TOO FINE.

WEAR CLOTHING THAT WILL BLEND WITH THE SURROUNDINGS, e.g. ARMY JACKET AND BUSH HAT.

**TERMINAL TACKLE**

IS BEST KEPT AS SIMPLE AS POSSIBLE WITH THE HOOK TIED DIRECTLY TO THE MAIN LINE. TOO MANY KNOTS MEAN WEAK POINTS, WHICH YOU CANNOT AFFORD, ESPECIALLY IF THE WATER IS HEAVILY WEEDED. THE WEIGHT OF THE BAIT IS USUALLY AMPLE TO MAKE CASTING EASY.

**METHOD OF TYING HOOK TO LINE.**

Pull tight and shave off end...

Size 4 Forged Hook.

...to achieve this.

**BAITS:** ARE NUMEROUS AND VARIED: BREAD (CRUST, FLAKE OR PASTE WITH HONEY IF DESIRED) LOBWORMS, REDWORMS, MAGGOTS, WASP GRUBS, SLUGS, SNAILS, FRESHWATER MUSSELS, BOILED POTATOES, CHEESE, MACARONI, SWEET CORN, AND VARIOUS MIXTURES OF HIGH PROTEIN BAIT, PLUS MANY MORE. BIG FISH SPECIALISTS USE MANY KINDS OF BEANS AND SEEDS.

POTATO SLICE TO OVERCOME SILK WEED OR SOFT MUD.

SWEET CORN.

**PRESENTATION**

BREAD PASTE MOULDED OVER HOOK.

TWO WAYS OF OVERCOMING SILK WEED OR SOFT MUD.

BREAD CRUST AND TINY BOMB.

CRUST AND PASTE. THREE OR FOUR LOBS.

SITE YOUR PITCH, IF POSSIBLE, WHERE THE SHALLOWS BEGIN TO DROP OFF INTO DEEPER WATER.

EARLY WARNING INDICATOR. FOLDED SILVER PAPER. LEAVE BALE ARM DISENGAGED.

FISHING OVER A PITCH WHICH HAS BEEN GROUND-BAITED FOR A PERIOD OF TWO OR THREE DAYS PRIOR TO FISHING IS LIKELY TO PROVE MORE PROFITABLE.

CARP SOON GET WISE TO A PARTICULAR BAIT, SO TRY AND FIND ONE WHICH HASN'T BEEN USED ON YOUR WATER.

4 a.m. SUMMER DAWN

CHOOSE A COMFORTABLE SEAT AS CARP FISHING IS USUALLY A WAITING GAME.

**GET READY**

ENGAGE BALE ARM WAIT FOR ANY SLACK LINE TO RUN OUT....

**STRIKE**

THE FIRST RUSH OF A HOOKED CARP IS FRIGHTENING AND THE ONLY WAY TO TURN A FISH WHICH IS HEADING FOR SNAGS IS TO WALK SOME DISTANCE ALONG THE BANK AND APPLY SIDE PRESSURE.

EXPECT TO BE BROKEN IF THE CARP FINDS A SOLID SNAG.

IF THE CARP HEADS FOR DEEPER WATER WHICH IS COMPARATIVELY SNAG FREE, LET HIM RUN, AND PLAY HIM OUT THERE RATHER THAN IN SHALLOWER WATER.

FISHING A FLOATING CRUST.

USE LILY PADS OR WEEDS WHERE EVER POSSIBLE, TO SCREEN AND ANCHOR LINE.

PUT YOUR CARP IN AN OPEN-WEAVE SACK WHERE HE WILL LIE STILL. AVOID CLOSE-WEAVE SACKS WHICH COULD SUFFOCATE THE FISH.

KITING: CAUSED BY THE FISH SWIMMING AT SUCH AN ANGLE, THAT THE PRESSURE APPLIED BY THE ANGLER BRINGS THE FISH IN A LARGE ARC AND HEADLONG INTO THE ANGLERS BANK AND SOME DISTANCE AWAY.

NIGHT FISHING IN MID SUMMER IS OFTEN THE MOST PROFITABLE, AND ON SOME OVERFISHED WATERS THE ONLY PRACTICAL TIME FOR A GOOD MEASURE OF SUCCESS.

... AND RETURN IT TO FIGHT ANOTHER DAY. DON'T ATTEMPT TO FISH THROUGH THE DAY, GO HOME AND GET SOME SLEEP......

AFTER A NIGHT SESSION PHOTOGRAPH YOUR CATCH...

YOU WILL NEED IT!

WHEN THE FISH IS IN THE NET, PUT YOUR ROD DOWN, GRASP THE MESH AND LIFT ONTO THE BANK, WELL CLEAR OF THE WATER.

BEWARE! OF THE CURSE KNOWN AS KITING — AN UNINTENTIONAL MOVE BY THE FISH, BUT THE RESULTS CAN BE SERIOUS.

LOWER THE CRUST GENTLY WHEN A CARP APPROACHES. THE LOOSE CRUST WILL BE TAKEN THEREBY SHOWING HIS POSITION.

MAKE SURE THERE IS ENOUGH SLACK LINE TO ALLOW THE BAIT TO BE SUCKED IN FREELY.

POSITION YOUR ITEMS OF TACKLE CLOSE AT HAND ON A GROUND SHEET.

THE IDEAL CARP NET HAS A HANDLE FIVE FEET LONG, A TRIANGULAR FRAME WITH THIRTY INCH ARMS, AND A STRONG MESH FOUR FEET DEEP.

PROBABLY THINKING THAT THE SMALLER PIECE IS A CRUMB, THE CARP USUALLY TAKES IT.

IF PESTERED BY SMALL FISH, RAISE THE BAIT ABOVE THE WATER LEVEL AND THROW IN A LOOSE CRUST.

TWO WAYS OF DETECTING A BITE AT NIGHT.

WHITE STICK.

ELECTRIC BITE INDICATOR.

REDUCE THE PRESSURE ON YOUR REEL CLUTCH AT THIS STAGE. WHEN THE CARP SEES THE NET IT MAY MAKE ONE LAST BID FOR FREEDOM. KEEP YOUR INDEX FINGER ON THE REEL SPOOL IN READINESS.

LARGE CRUST THREADED ON THE LINE.

SMALL CRUST ON HOOK.

....SO TRY THIS

TAKE ADVANTAGE OF BANK-SIDE COVER.

IF A LIGHT IS USED ALWAYS KEEP IT POINTING AWAY FROM THE WATER.

SHINE THE LIGHT ON THE WATER ONLY IN AN EMERGENCY e.g., LANDING A BIG FISH.

THERE ARE TIMES WHEN CARP WILL TURN OFF A CRUST OR JUST NIBBLE THE EDGES......

HERE AGAIN USE A FLOATING CRUST ABOUT TWO INCHES SQUARE.

BEFORE BRINGING A CARP TO THE NET, MAKE SURE IT IS BEATEN AND ON ITS SIDE.

**MARGIN FISHING**
CARP WILL OFTEN PATROL VERY CLOSE TO THE BANK, USUALLY EARLY IN THE MORNING OR ON WARM SUMMER NIGHTS.
THESE FISH ARE ON THE LOOKOUT FOR ANY TIT BITS THEY CAN FIND. THE BEST AREA TO TRY THIS METHOD IS THE END OF THE LAKE INTO WHICH THE WIND IS BLOWING.

HOWEVER IT IS NOT A GAME FOR NOVICES TO INDULGE IN SINGLE HANDED.

SUMMER NIGHTS CAN BE VERY COLD. WRAP UP WELL AND TAKE PLENTY OF FOOD AND HOT DRINK.

SUNSET.

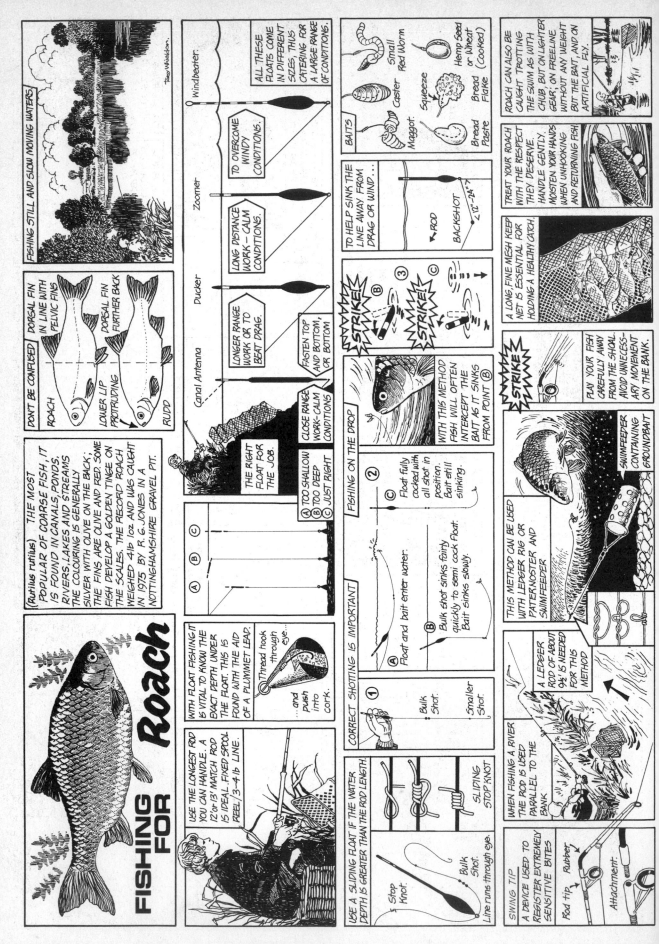

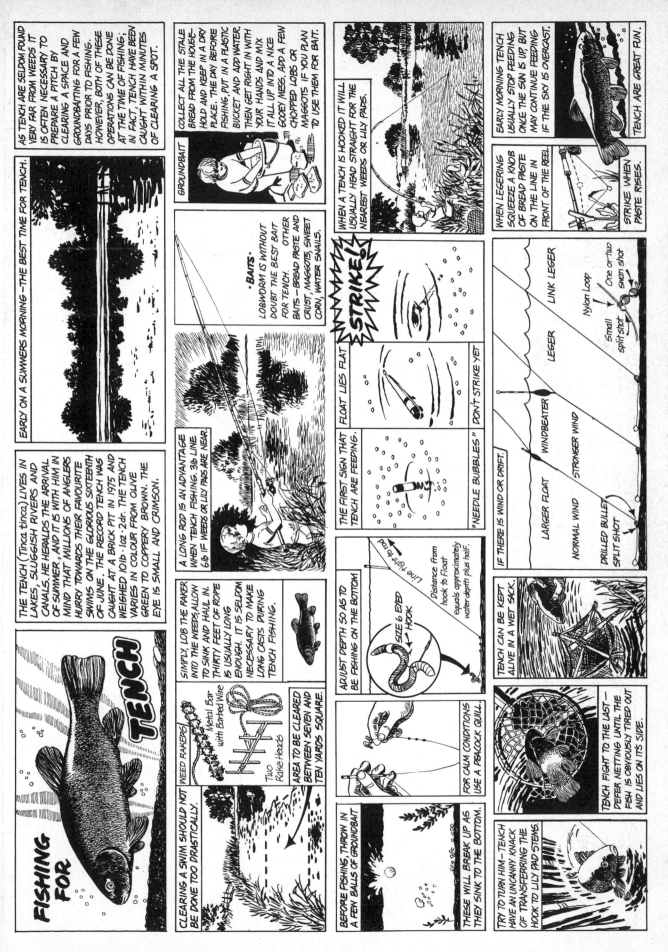

# It pays to be a 'Peeping Tom'!
## says JOHN BAILEY

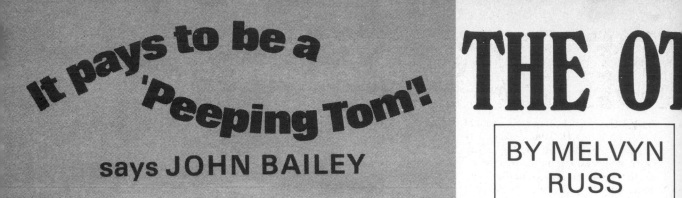

# THE OT

## BY MELVYN RUSS

BIG fish are difficult enough to catch but I give myself the best possible chance by observing their behaviour whenever I can. Then I think about what I've seen and try to put my observations to good use.

There are several swims in my local rivers and lakes where I can watch the fish and learn from them. The river here is a little-used backwater of the Wensum and generally flows slow and clear. A spinney keeps the wind from the water and gives me the cover I need to get to the bank.

Basically, the swim holds roach, perch, pike. It is typical of small river swims and is the holding area for a large stretch of water. The roach form a large shoal for the river, perhaps 60 to 70. A fair percentage, say 20 per cent, are $1\frac{1}{2}$ lb. or over, with a few going close to 2 lb.

In summer these fish feed fairly constantly. They roll at dawn in the shallows, then come back into the deeper water and feed spasmodically through the day. The larger roach take a considerable amount of time to start feeding properly but after three quarters of a pint of maggots have been thrown in, the pound-plus fish sometimes begin to pick them up. Even then, they are unlikely to take them in mid-winter and certainly never, in my experience, while on a hook!

In the slow current of the bend a trotted maggot looks quite different from a free-falling one, even to me—so goodness knows what it looks like to a roach. The only time I've seen big roach take trotted maggots happily was in a faster swim where a submerged pipe caused a turbulence that swept all the maggots spiralling upwards, hooked or not. In a slow swim like this the maggot must be hard on the bottom.

As with maggots, bread is treated with suspicion at first. I think there is a definite case for pre-baiting here, for if large roach haven't seen bread for some time there is a decided reluctance to take it at all. After steady but sparing feeding over two to three days, even the largest fish will take bread avidly and on the drop, as the heavier bread falls more easily than maggots.

These fish are a difficult proposition in winter. When the water temperature drops below 36 or 37°F. they will not move for food at all, although any increase in water temperature, however slight, might well put them back on the feed. Maggots brushing right up against their mouths may be sucked in. This explains why you can work a swim over and over again without success and then suddenly get a bite.

A warm, drizzly day seems to activate the roach shoal most—and when the river is fining down from flood, if the weather has previously been very sharp, even the large fish will feed well. But even then, it is amazing how many "free" maggots large roach will suck in and then spit out very quickly. On several occasions I have seen big roach chewing only one in six of the maggots they originally took. But an angler would not see any indication on his float and no mark left on the maggot.

The perch are also slow to feed but for different reasons. These are big fish of around $2\frac{1}{2}$ lb. and very much like pike in the way they lie comatose until something triggers off their feeding interest. I have frequently thrown lobworm after lobworm past them but had them ignored and seen them eaten by the smaller perch that seem much more consistently alert for food. But throw a very small livebait to a good perch and the chances of a take are much greater.

Unless these big perch are obviously in a feeding mood, moving round the hole, chasing small fish and so on, there is very little chance of maggots ever being taken. The fact that they feed rarely and need a definite stimulus to start at all is one reason why big perch are seldom caught, even from a fishery with a good stock of them.

My swim also holds four pike, two of which are big. I caught one of 15 lb. and the second is only a little smaller. The other two are "jacks", but occasionally I see a good fish of about 10 lb. in the swim for a day or two and then she leaves.

Like the perch, these pike lie completely still for days. They seem to eat irregularly, especially in winter. I could throw three herrings in on Monday and they'll still be there on Wednesday. But on Thursday all three will have gone. Perhaps live fish are taken between times, but why should they?

At first I was struck by what I thought was the illogical behaviour of the fish I watched, but I soon realised it was for a purpose. Frequently, for example, the perch corkscrewed into the gravel and mud of the bed and sent up clouds of debris. They would then turn quickly and sift through the falling material for food.

Similarly, whenever roach primed the surface it was just a preliminary to going down to feed. When a shoal of smaller fish becomes agitated, it generally precedes a feeding spell of the perch.

You need patience to be an angling "Peeping Tom". But what will you gain by fishing in the same old way every time you go out, never really knowing the creatures you're hunting?

Ray in action at a Surrey lake, playing a carp to the waiting landing net.

RAY MUMFORD has won national fame as a match-fishing expert. A bright shining star on the big-money Open competition circuit. But there's another side to this colourful Londoner that very few anglers know—Mumford the specimen hunter.

Ray never fails to add a little spice to a match, either because of the way he fishes or because of his outspoken views. But he keeps one aim firmly in mind and that is to catch big fish when he slips away during the week for a quiet afternoon or two out of the public eye.

His job as a printer provides the flexible working hours needed for midweek pleasure-fishing for big roach on his local stretch of the River Thames at Kingston—or tucked away in a leafy corner of a gravel pit, coaxing a carp to take a floating crust.

"The great thing about specimen fishing is that I can try where I like for any species I fancy without the pressure of someone trying to beat me," says Ray, who has been clocking up match wins since he was a teenager.

He is not obsessed by any particular fish. So long as it's big and gives a good fight, that's fair enough. But he likes to give them all a sporting chance by fishing "light".

Ray is one of a growing band of anglers who believe that heavy tackle belongs to the past and considers that tackle used by some pike and carp men should be left at home.

He puts his views like this: "Anyone can reel in a weighty fish on beefy tackle but where's the sport in that? Many anglers take the wrong approach to specimen fishing. They seem to think that 20 lb. line for piking is the norm. Well, so far as I am concerned, those breaking strains are for sea fishing.

"Fish are not stupid. They are

(Above) Ray's angling workhorse is a bright green van, fitted out to take all his tackle and the vast range of baits he uses when match and pleasure fishing.
(Below)
This near double-figure mirror carp fell for Ray Mumford's bread-flake and was played out on a match rod.

A good-condition winter bream caught in a gravel pit at Staines, Middlesex.

becoming wiser as waters buckle under the pressure of modern day angling. So the fish are now very wary and the only way to catch them is to present a bait that looks as natural as it is possible to make it.

"A light line and small barbless hooks will always catch more fish than conventional rigs. Every time I see a pike angler heaving out half a mackerel on beachcasting gear I have a little chuckle."

Ray is an exponent of the "light approach". And when he says light he means it. For him, a 5 lb. line for carp fishing is nothing out of the ordinary and 10 lb. is maximum for pike lines.

Perhaps the most impressive aspect of Mumford the specimen hunter is the way he has taken the vast knowledge gained on the tough match circuit and turned it to his advantage on those quiet afternoons away from it all.

I have watched Ray trying patiently to tempt a double-figure carp with a 12 ft. hollowglass rod, float tackle and piece of breadflake. It may sound ludicrous to a hardened carp angler—but it works and there are very few fish that get away from him.

The same goes for pike fishing. Ray doesn't go so far as to fish for them with a match rod but he's had a pair of specially light rods made up for piking. And, again, it's the light approach that always seems to score. His pike bungs are tiny, never more than two inches long and three quarters of an inch wide. Lines average about 8 lb. or

**Ray was well pleased with this bag of pike, all lured by tiny livebaits.**

10 lb. with a tiny pair of trebles on a home-made trace to complete the outfit. He uses very small livebaits and tends to favour dace, roach and bleak.

He fishes with two pike rods, but close together so that he can keep a watchful eye on both. He doesn't like what he calls "factory fishing", where anglers string out up to six rods and sit back and wait. Ray is a worker who likes to search out every likely-looking lie with livebaits before moving swims.

The settings of his float are changed frequently so that the bait explores varying depths. Likewise, rods and baits are moved gradually over a period of time until he is satisfied the whole area has been covered.

When a pike takes, there are no amateur dramatics from Ray. No counting up to 20 before whipping back the rod in a full arc. That's not the Mumford style. He makes a clean hooking by gently tightening the line and calmly lifting the rod until the hook sets.

The same unflustered approach is used for bream fishing. This is a branch of the sport where Ray's match-fishing knowledge really helps with groundbaiting patterns, timing and accuracy that play so great a part in successful bream sessions—but can only be learned with practice.

Ask Ray Mumford to put a series of balls of groundbait into a two-foot wide circle, six rodlengths out on a blustery day, and it's as good as done. Only constant practice over a period of time can make you that good.

Ray's choice of a bream outfit comprises a nine-foot leger rod, fitted with a lengthy swingtip. A smallish hook baited with bread, worm, or maggots and caster is used to attract the fish

**A small pike caught on a tiny bleak.**

and an Arlesey bomb gets the business end into the target area.

When a fish moves the swingtip up comes the rod in a gentle sweeping movement and the fish is on. Any sudden rushes are softened by the top end of the rod but the first thing Ray tries to do is get the bream away from the shoal.

Ray is full of stories about his long and interesting career in coarse fishing. But the tale I like is about a day in 1955 when he was fishing with cheese for Hampshire Avon barbel but hooked a 22 lb. pike.

"I remember every minute of that fight to this day," recalls Ray. "I was using only 7 lb. line and the pike's first rush tangled me up in a load of weeds. My first reaction was 'record barbel' or even a whacking big salmon. I had to follow the fish downstream and scramble over a bridge before I could see it was a pike!"

## RAY MUMFORD'S LOG OF SPECIMENS

**Mirror carp** 20¼ lb., Hampshire lake.
**Pike** 22 lb., Hampshire Avon.
**Barbel** 12 lb. 6 oz., Hampshire Avon.
**Bream** 6¼ lb., Knight and Besborough reservoir.
**Chub** 6 lb., Hampshire Avon.
**Roach** 2 lb. 8 oz., Barn Elms reservoir.
**Tench** 5½ lb., Leisure Sport's Wraysbury No. 1 lake.
**Crucian carp,** 2½ lb., Farnborough pit.
**Salmon** 20 lb., Hampshire Avon.
**Rainbow trout** 16 lb., Avington, Winchester.
**Brown trout** 7½ lb., Cirencester lake.
**Sea trout** 8½ lb., Hampshire lake.

A fine bag of bream taken from Walthamstow reservoir, London, on caster and maggot.

The one that didn't get away. Ray admires the 22 lb. Avon pike he caught on cheese!

# Holidays Afloat

## by Harry Arnold

If you've never been able to persuade the family to come fishing, hiring a boat could provide just the key to luring them down to the water. Especially when your wife discovers that many modern inland waterway cruisers contain all the comforts of home—a full-size cooker, refrigerator, hot and cold running water, shower, central heating and even television! On the surface, there is a basic conflict between angling and boating on restricted waterways as you've probably noticed when another passing boat disturbs your fishing, but with a little tolerance and good sense on both sides this can be reduced to a minimum.

Almost 3,500 miles of canals and rivers in England, Scotland and Wales are navigable by craft on which you can live aboard. These waterways are survivors of a network of over 5,000 miles built as artificial canals or made navigable as the commercial arteries of the industrial revolution. Unlike other European countries, where waterways are used extensively for the carriage of heavy goods, the major boating use of Britain's rivers and canals is pleasure cruising.

Due to peculiarities of geography and history, the network can be divided roughly into three major parts—the Norfolk Broads, the Thames and the narrow canal and river system of the Midlands.

The Broads, where holiday cruising really developed between the two World Wars, are not connected physically to the rest of the system. Pleasure boating also has a long history on the Thames, due to its proximity to London. The rest comprises a network of mostly inter-connected canals and rivers stretching north from the Thames to link the Severn, Mersey, Trent, Humber and the Wash. Some are totally isolated or reached only by a tidal passage, such as the Brecon and Abergavenny Canal in South Wales, the River Medway in Kent or the Lancaster Canal in North Lancashire. Equally separate are the Caledonian and Crinan Canals in Scotland.

A modern narrow-beam hire cruiser on the Trent & Mersey Canal near Lichfield.

Even the connected network has its complications. Due to varying ideas and economics, waterways were built to different "gauges" with the central canal system of the Midlands built to take the well-known "narrow boat", with locks of 70 feet long by 7 feet wide. Other waterways were built with wider locks of 14 feet and over but, to confuse matters, sometimes shorter than 70 feet. The great Midland system, stretching from Oxford to Chester and the Welsh Border, and largely controlled by the British Waterways Board, has shown the great development in waterway holidays over the last ten years. Many new fleets of custom-built, narrow-beam, hire cruisers have been established, particularly on and around the Shropshire Union and Oxford Canals.

There is no better way of exploring Britain's countryside than travelling by boat. Contrary to the much held popular belief, most of our rivers and canals are not dirty and polluted and very few miles of them pass through urban areas. The majority wend through peaceful and often spectacular scenery, away from the noise of the roads and the rush and bustle of modern life. With so many miles of waterway to cruise, at an average speed of about 4 miles per hour, and with comparatively short holidays, the choice is endless.

Should it be the Broads with 200 miles of rivers and wide shallow lakes—plus, if you like, the bright lights and seaside of Great Yarmouth? Then there's England's Royal River, the Thames—124 miles of liquid history from London to Lechlade, climbing steadily to the Cotswolds by 45 mechanised locks past Hampton Court, Runnymede, Windsor and Oxford.

Radiating from the Wash are the Fenland waterways, another 200 miles of colourful cruising connected to the main network by the River Nene, but really, like the Broads, a compact system on their own.

But there are still another 2,000 miles from which to choose . . . The vast spread of the central canal and river system, extending northwards and westwards to Merseyside, Lancashire, Yorkshire and Wales and criss-crossing the Midland counties with a maze of man-made water highways. These canals are the work of some of England's greatest civil engineers such as Brindley, Jessop and Telford. Men who were not only engineers but artists in brick, stone and iron. Their cuts, bridges and buildings blend into the countryside and have their own special character. Unlike rivers, the canals do not stick to the valleys, but climb over hills by flights of locks and burrow through them by long, cool tunnels. High embankments and aqueducts carry them across the valleys. To look down from a boat from Telford's 120 feet high Pontcycyllte Aqueduct on to the Dee Valley below is a unique and long-remembered experience.

The choice is difficult. Every canal and river has its own special attraction. Top of the league in popularity are the Llangollen and Oxford Canals, followed closely by the main line of the Shropshire Union, the Stratford Canal and the re-opened Shakespeare's River Avon. Everyone has a special favourite and few, if any, will disappoint you. Remember, too, that because most of the central network is inter-connected, circular one-way cruises are possible as well as the usual out-and-return variety.

Yorkshire's waterways are wide and often still busy with commercial craft, so you will find few pleasure boats as yet. Connecting these over the Pennines is the grand Leeds & Liverpool Canal, a waterway of splendid contrasts. Apart from the Llangollen Canal, the only other survivor of a once-extensive system in Wales is the Brecon & Abergavenny. This isolated little canal is in a National Park for most of its length and is a true gem.

Scotland has one of the great spectaculars of inland cruising, the Caledonian Canal. Built as a sea-to-sea ship canal, the Caledonian follows the mountainous Highland cleft of the Great Glen, joining together the inland lakes of Loch Ness, Loch Oich and Loch Lochy. These areas of water are so big, and often deep, that it is often more akin to sea boating.

**Crossing Edstone Aqueduct on the Stratford-upon-Avon Canal.**

**Napton Locks on the Oxford Canal.**

But what about the boats? Because of the varying "gauge" of the waterways the boats fall into two basic types: narrow beam, under 7 feet wide and capable of negotiating the locks of the narrow canals; and wide beam, over 7 feet wide and generally used on waters such as the Thames, Broads and Fens.

So, remember, if you hire a boat from a yard on a river like the Thames and wish to include the connected narrow canals in your holiday the boat must be narrow beam. Wide beam river cruisers are generally styled on sea-going boats and almost invariably steered with a wheel. The steering position may be in a centre cockpit, with a folding wheelhouse or canopy, or in a completely enclosed forward position in the main cabin structure as in the new generation of hire cruisers developed on the Broads.

Because of its lack of width, a narrow beam boat must necessarily be more compact in internal layout; but you will find that the canal boat-builders have overcome this by ingenious utilisation of available space. The other big difference you will notice with the majority of modern canal hire cruisers is that they are steered with a tiller at the stern and their hull shape is generally based on that of the traditional working narrow boat. The tiller may look an unfamiliar object compared with the wheel, which is similar to your car, but it really is the best method of steering a boat. A "touch" immediately corrects the boat's course and the helmsman's position gives a clear view of all of the

craft. Hulls of canal boats are also usually made of steel to stand up to the inevitable bumps and scrapes in the narrow locks. It is possible to hire wheel-steered craft on canals but these are becoming fewer.

Where the larger wide and narrow beam boats do not differ is in the standard of their fittings and equipment. The average holidaymakers, especially the ladies, are demanding "all mod. cons." and with the rapid strides in boatbuilding techniques these can be provided. Full-size single and double beds, hot and cold running water, showers, flush toilets, gas or electric refrigerators, full household-size gas cookers, central heating or individual cabin heaters and television—all are now common features. Your boat will also have a full inventory of all the loose equipment required for your holiday. All you will need to bring are towels, tea cloths and your own personal belongings.

What do you need to know? Very little really. The hire company will teach you how to steer the boat and operate its equipment, the Do's and Don'ts of cruising and how to work a lock. The majority of locks on the waterways are operated by the boat's crew. This is a simple and mildly energetic exercise and nothing to be afraid of. If you want to read it up and plan your route beforehand there is a wide choice of books on the subject. For general reading, *The Canals Book*, *The Thames Book* and *The Broads Book* are excellent. General maps of the waterways are produced by Hoseasons, Stanfords and Imray, Laurie, Norie & Wilson. For blow by blow use on the boat, showing you

every lock, pub, shop or boatyard, you need the *Nicholsons Guides to the Waterways* for the canals and the Thames, or the large scale maps of the Broads published by the major booking agencies, Hoseasons and Blakes. Many other publications are available, usually obtainable from a local large bookshop, library, or the company with whom you book.

How much will it cost you? A generalisation is difficult because of differences in the size of boat, facilities offered and time of year. On a price per head basis, the 1978 rate for a luxury 8-berth narrow beam cruiser varies from £15 per person per week out of season to £32 per week in the peak season, plus VAT. Watch out for extras. Firms are tending to go over to "all inclusive" charges but fuel is still likely to be charged on top. Hire cruisers are increasingly going over to diesel power. Petrol engines are thirsty and the price of petrol is just the same on the water as on the road. Gas oil can be used in a diesel engine boat.

A diesel engine is very economical in consumption and the fuel is cheap. The boat can also carry enough fuel to run for weeks without refilling, so the answer is obvious. Watch out for the low basic hire fee, plus extras for tolls, gas, and so on. When you add it up this can come to more than the inclusive price.

Insurance on the boat will be in the price but you will be expected to pay a Damage Deposit of about £30 per boat. This is returnable in full if you don't damage the boat or lose any of its equipment.

Licence and toll fees are usually included but there are slight complica-

Crossing Loch Ness on the Caledonian Canal.

**Young anglers and boats on Oulton Broad, Suffolk.**

Anyone hiring a boat through Hoseasons during this period (October 4 to 18 in 1978) has free entry in a competition for the best roach, bream, pike or perch caught. There are various categories, including Juniors and Ladies, with over £300 in prizes to be won.

Who can you book with? There are hundreds of firms hiring out boats but I can list only a few.

**Anglo-Welsh Narrow Boats,** The Canal Basin, Leicester Road, Market Harborough, Leics. LE16 7BJ. Tel: Market Harborough 2594—Over 80 boats on the canals, operating from a choice of five bases.

**Boat Enquiries Ltd,** 7 Walton Well Road, Oxford OX2 6ED. Tel: Oxford 511555—Booking service for most waterways.

**Blakes (Norfolk Broads Holidays) Ltd,** Wroxham, Norwich NR12 8DH. Tel: Wroxham 2141—Central booking agency handling 1,200 boats on the Broads and 300 on the Thames and Canals.

**Caley Cruisers,** Muirtown, Inverness, Scotland. Tel: Inverness 36328—The major hire fleet on the Caledonian Canal.

**Hoseasons Holidays,** Sunway House, Lowestoft, Suffolk NR32 3LT. Tel: Lowestoft 62181, 67511 & 66622—Central booking agency handling 1,050 boats on the Broads and 1,100 boats on the Thames and Canals.

tions on the Midland canals. Short, odd stretches of waterway are owned by bodies such as the National Trust and as the hire company does not know if you are going to navigate these as part of your route you may be expected to pay the extra toll required, on top of the British Waterways Board licence included in the hire fee.

Other tips . . . Book early—waterway holidays are very popular. If possible go and look at the boat beforehand. That glossy brochure picture may not be what it seems. On the other hand, remember that when you call to take a look the boat may be out of commission, stripped of its equipment and undergoing major servicing for the coming season. It may require some imagination to compare it in this condition, on a cold winter day, with living aboard in summer! There are no national standards for the operation of hire cruisers but on the Thames the Water Authority sets standards of safety for all craft licensed by them. Standards are set by trade associations and booking agencies on the Broads and on the canals by the Association of Pleasure Craft Operators. Check if a company is a member of a trade association when you book.

# WHEN TO GO

The season now stretches from early March to early November and some firms hire all the year round—including Christmas. My preference is May, but unfortunately this is the Close Season for coarse fishing. Of particular interest to anglers is Hoseasons "Anglers Fortnight".

*Holidays Afloat was first printed in "Fishing Holidays Guide", published by Angler's Mail in 1975, updated and revised with new illustrations for Angler's Mail Annual 1980 by Harry Arnold.*

PICTURES: MIKE MILLMAN (PORBEAGLE) ANON. (MAKO)

# Jaws!

Shark fishing in British waters is now so well-organised, including its own specialist club based at Looe, Cornwall, that every season produces "Jaws"-style stories for the National newspapers. This toothsome head of a porbeagle shark was photographed soon after its capture off Crackington Haven, North Cornwall, where many outsize porbeagles have fallen to rod and line, including the World Record specimen of 465 lb.

Head of a 260 lb. mako shark, caught at Islamorado, Florida Keys, America. The British mako record is 500 lb., caught by another well-known woman angler, Mrs Joyce Yallop, on a trip to Eddystone Reef, Devon, in 1971.

WHEN Angler's Mail recruited a party of prominent specimen hunters for a fact-finding mission at the northern end of Loch Lomond they saw plenty of pike action, three golden eagles and herds of wild deer.

These are some of the highlights of the trip captured by photographer Ron Felton and discussed by Roy Westwood.

RIGHT . . . A morning's catch of pike from the popular, shallow grounds at Ardlui. From left: Barrie Rickards, Mick Edkins, boatman Andy Finlayson and Hugh Reynolds.

EXTREME RIGHT . . . The Lomond safari produced an unexpected bonus in the shape of this 16 lb. brown trout for Barrie Rickards. It is thought to be the best from the loch since the turn of the century and was taken on a wobbled plug.

Lomond can be as dangerous as the open sea and our band of pike hunters tuned in to the shipping forecasts so they had fair warning of bad weather brewing. But if conditions deteriorate it's always possible to seek sanctuary in one of the many sheltered bays dotted around the loch shores like this secluded corner. The boats were provided by the Arrochar BHC and their mobility contributed greatly to the success of the trip.

LEFT . . . With the snow-covered peaks forming a rugged backcloth, a Loch Lomond pike shatters the surface in its bid for freedom.

Pier fishing has attracted generations of anglers; countless thousands wet their first sea-fishing lines at the end of one of the ornate Victorian shore extensions that housed (in season) concert parties, amusement arcades, fortune tellers, penny peepshows and the like. But the ravages of time, and the high cost of repairs and maintenance, have steadily reduced the number of piers and anglers are among the main losers. This view of pier fishing at Douglas, Isle of Man, captures the windswept pleasures of a cast over the rails.

A 22 lb. Cuttle Mill carp, displayed by captor Ron Felton, of Birmingham. Cuttle Mill, near Tamworth, Staffs., is a day-ticket fishery run by Albert Brewer. Many carp anglers have caught their first 20-pounders here and it has been among the most consistent water for quality fish in recent years. As the majority of carp waters are in the hands of syndicates, Cuttle Mill's ticket facilities are very popular.

PICTURE: ANGLER'S MAIL LIBRARY

Floatplanes and a fleet of fast angling launches operate from Red's Camp, La Ronge, to carry anglers to fishing grounds favoured by Cree Indian guides. The 'planes are available for transfers to other popular lake centres in Northern Saskatchewan.

# FISHING IN CANADA'S FAR NORTH

Cree Indian guides . . . modern motels with colour TVs . . . and 500 square miles of fabulous fishing. It's all happening at La Ronge, once a Hudson's Bay trading post and now a thriving angling centre in northern Saskatchewan.

An American visitor and his Indian guide are off the mark with a pickerel—but hoping for one of the lake's monster trout.

A powerful 30 h.p. outboard motor lifts the bows of a Red's Camp launch as a day's outing comes to an end and anglers head for their modern motel on the lake shore.

As recently as 1946, the historic settlement of La Ronge, in Canada's northern Saskatchewan, was virtually isolated as a community of hunters, fishermen, trappers and a Cree Indian Reservation. But La Ronge is now a thriving centre with 3,000 residents and a bustling seasonal population of tourists. The main attraction for anglers is Lac La Ronge, a vast water of about 500 square miles, dotted with more than a thousand islands and offering some of the best walleye (pickerel), northern pike and lake trout fishing in the world. Our pictures show some of the action on Lac La Ronge when Angler's Mail joined a party of journalists and British travel experts on Air Canada's first direct flight from London to Saskatoon. A feature article on La Ronge and Saskatchewan will be found in other pages of the Annual.

PICTURES: ANGLER'S MAIL LIBRARY AND DOUGLAS DICKENS

**RIGHT: Adam, a Cree Indian fishing guide, is a highly respected personality at La Ronge and displays a handsome lake trout that fell for his baited spoon. BELOW: A camp-fire picnic lunch for an angling party on one of the thousand islands in Lac La Ronge. The pickerel in the frying pans were caught less than an hour earlier. BELOW (right): Sue Burr, a Berkshire travel agent, and Merv Johnson, Agent General in London for the Provincial Government of Saskatchewan, admire some of the fish caught by a visiting party of journalists and travel agents.**

Ray Mumford has achieved national fame as a top performer in the highly competitive world of match-fishing, where the stakes are high and the pressure correspondingly intense. But little has been written about Ray's quiet hours spent on fishing for fun and relaxation. Our pictures show Ray enjoying an outing on a Berkshire river and (inset) the end of a good day as Ray prepares to return a catch of barbel. Elsewhere in this edition of Angler's Mail Annual, you will find a special article by Melvyn Russ on The Other Ray Mumford—away from it all.

PICTURES: ANGLER'S MAIL LIBRARY

# TACKLING UP FOR SEA FISH

## By Peter Grundel

Most manufacturers label their rods with the recommended best range of casting weights for each of their models—but the type of shoreline to be fished must also be taken into account, advises Peter Grundel.

UNLIKE boat fishing, where tackle is lowered to the bottom, a beachcasting outfit must be capable of propelling a bait towards the horizon. So the choice of rod and reel is crucial and the correct combination will depend largely on the topography of the shore.

For example, a winter cod outfit selected for the dense kelp jungles on the Yorkshire coast would prove less than ideal for a sheltered sandy West Country cove. Equally, the powerful equipment needed to punch out a big lead in the fast scouring tides along the Kent coast would be too combersome for most estuaries.

On open, deep water and tide-swept shores, a 5-6 oz. rod is necessary. This is particularly true when facing prevailing winds. Typical of these shores are the steep-to beaches at Deal and Dungeness and several of the Suffolk stations.

Then there are the sandy, surf beaches along the western side of Britain where long, cresting breakers roll in from afar to pummel the sands. Waves on these shores appear more spectacular than the short, steep waves which hit a shingle beach. But they are not afflicted by the scouring tides found farther east in the bottleneck of the English Channel and can be fished with a much lighter rod, designed to cast leads in the 3-4 oz. range.

An even lighter rod, for use with leads up to a maximum of 2 oz., is admirable for more sheltered waters in bays, coves and estuaries—especially over a clean bottom of sand or mud.

For all practical purposes, there's no need to look further than hollow fibreglass for the basic material of a good beachcasting rod. Solid glass is too heavy and the expense and restricted choice of models tends to rule out carbon fibre.

Most manufacturers recommend the best range of casting weights for each of their models. From this information, and taking into consideration the sort of shoreline you will be fishing, a rod of the correct casting weight can then be selected.

Rods specifically designed for this type of work vary from 10 ft. to more than 14 ft. in length. There are advantages to be gained from the longer weapons but remember that no rod casts by itself—YOU have to provide the propulsion. Many anglers over-reach themselves in this respect. A muscular six-footer may comfortably handle the big rods but those of more modest physique would be wise to settle for the models between 11 ft. and 12 ft.

Experienced beach fishermen tend to confuse newcomers by arguing the merits, or otherwise, of fast taper, medium taper and slow-actioned rods. To clarify the situation, stiff rods with a fast action are rather more efficient at powering out the lead but slower-action models are more tolerant of any imperfections in casting technique.

But any design and taper of modern beachcasting rod is capable of depositing the lead long distances, provided it is used by a proficient caster. So there is a great deal more to be gained from acquiring a good casting technique than from becoming involved in the complexities of rod design.

# REELS

This free-spool multiplying reel, fitted with a plastic spool, is suitable for beachcasting. A quick take-apart sideplate to enable spools to be changed in a few seconds is also a desirable feature.

A fixed-spool reel used in conjunction with a line release. Casting with leads exceeding 3 oz. can be extremely painful for the forefinger but a line release, which is attached to the rod butt as shown in the picture, holds the line firmly in place until it is released.

REELS for beach work fall into two distinct categories— fixed-spool and revolving drum. But quite apart from mechanical excellence, any reel is only as good as its back-up service. That is why easily obtainable spares are vitally important.

Fixed-spool reels for beachcasting are basically similar but bigger than their freshwater counterparts. Provided the spool is correctly filled to within $\frac{1}{8}$ in. from the lip of the drum, casting is comparatively straightforward.

This type of reel is excellent for night fishing, when the risk of a "birdsnest" is greatest. It also scores when recovering terminal tackle across snaggy ground as the recovery rate of a fixed-spool is generally superior to that of a multiplier. On the debit side, a fixed-spool is more cumbersome than a multiplier of equivalent capacity and bail arm mechanisms are easily broken or bent out of line.

Fixed-spools also need a great deal more maintenance, as they possess numerous nooks and crannies where saltwater can seep in to cause corrosion.

Heavy lines over 20 lb. make a poor combination with fixed spools, as the large diameter of these lines means the drum loading drops down quickly during casting—and the ine soon forms a right angle where it runs over the lip. This causes a great deal of friction and subsequent loss of distance.

If you need to cast a big lead with this type of reel, it is better to load up with 15-18 lb. line, to which is knotted a 20 ft. length of 30-40 lb. monofil. This absorbs the stresses of casting but allows the use of a line of moderate diameter.

Casting with leads exceeding 3 oz. can be extremely painful on the forefinger and I recommend the use of a line release. These are attached on the rod butt and hold the line firmly in place until it is released.

A free-spool multiplying reel, with its fast revving drum spewing off line at a terrific rate during the cast, conjures up all sorts of terrors for those who have never used them. Mastery of a multiplier is certainly far less easy to achieve than with a fixed-spool reel but, at the same time, a multiplying reel offers advantages which should be seriously considered.

Firstly, this type of reel is far less cumbersome and much less prone to damage than its fixed-spool equivalent. Distance losses through line friction are minimised because the line runs directly off the revolving drum and straight through the rod rings without forming an angle.

It also follows that a greater range of line diameters may be employed efficiently and if you should lose several yards of line by snagging on the bottom, casting range will not be greatly impaired.

But, unlike fixed-spools, not all multipliers are suitable for casting. It is essential to obtain a casting reel and not one which has been designed for boat work.

The most important feature of a good casting multiplier is the spool. This needs to be as light as possible in order to minimise the problems of inertia. The lighter the spool, the easier it becomes to set it rolling and, conversely, the easier it is to stop with your thumb at the end of the cast, and so prevent excess line spewing out to form a birdsnest.

Spools constructed from heavy materials such as chrome-plated brass, are entirely unsuitable for casting purposes. So make sure the model you choose has a spool made from a lightweight material, such as fibreglass, plastic or anodised aluminium.

A quick, take-apart sideplate, which enables spools to be changed in a matter of seconds without the annoyance of loose screws falling out all over the beach, is also a

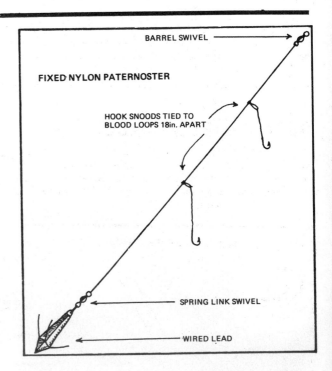

This multiplier is fitted with a heavy chrome brass spool, is fine for boat-fishing but, says the author, it is entirely unsuitable for beach fishing.

desirable feature.

A smooth, judder-free slipping clutch also helps, but the advantages bestowed by level wind mechanisms are more open to debate. Certainly, this type of device functions efficiently, laying the line smoothly and evenly across the drum, but I find that few people encounter much difficulty in mastering the knack of laying the line manually with the aid of the thumb.

Level wind mechanisms also become traps for wind-blown sand and they are not easily cleaned on the beach. In theory, the extra gears needed to drive the level wind gate backwards and forwards across the face of the reel impair the casting performance. But in practice I find that distance losses are minimal.

# 3 BASIC RIGS

THREE basic terminal rigs are adequate for most occasions when bottom fishing from the shore. These can be modified slightly to suit conditions or species and are simple to make.

I am not a believer in swarms of swivels and other iron-mongery as the diagrams demonstrate.

## FIXED NYLON PATERNOSTERS

Ideal in strong currents or when the sea is rough and coloured. Fish hit the bait forcefully and hang on rather longer than in calmer waters. This is my favourite tackle for winter cod and whiting, and for bass on more surfy beaches.

Make the rig by introducing one, two or three small bloodloops about 18 in. apart into a length of stout nylon. Eight-inch lengths of lighter nylon are tied to each loop and suitable hooks attached. A strong, spring link swivel is tied at the bottom of the trace for attaching the lead. At the other end is a barrel swivel for joining the trace to the reel line.

Hook sizes will depend on bait and species but in rough conditions there is little virtue in using tiny hooks.

My general guide: 3/0 to 6/0 for bass and cod; 1 and 1/0 for whiting and 2/0 to 4/0 for flatfish.

I normally use this rig with a lead incorporating anchor

**FIXED NYLON PATERNOSTER**

BARREL SWIVEL

HOOK SNOODS TIED TO BLOOD LOOPS 18in. APART

SPRING LINK SWIVEL

WIRED LEAD

wires because fish tend to locate their food by smell in rough, coloured seas. They can do this more easily if the bait is tethered instead of rolling about the sea bed.

# RUNNING NYLON PATERNOSTERS

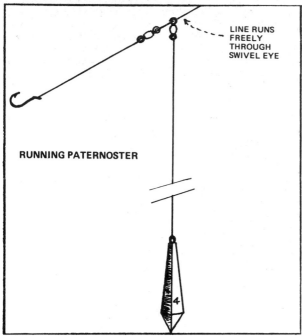

RUNNING PATERNOSTER

LINE RUNS FREELY THROUGH SWIVEL EYE

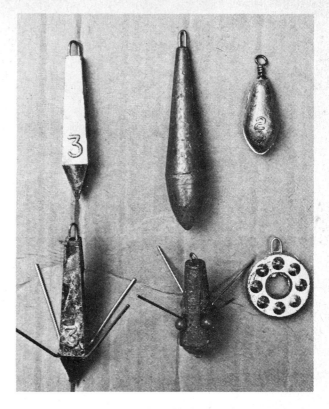

Shore fishing leads . . . flat-sided torpedo, smooth torpedo, Arlesey bomb, spiked torpedo, breakway lead and watch lead.

The running nylon paternoster allows a fish mouthing the bait to take line, providing the rod-tip is dropped after the first indication of a bite.

This rig is useful for shy species in calm conditions and comes into its own when fishing large baits, such as a whole crab or big pieces of fish.

On these occasions it is possible to pay out line and delay the strike until the bait is completely inside the mouth of the fish.

I tie a weak nylon link to the sinker over snaggy ground for obvious reasons. But it pays to impart some movement to the bait over relatively snag-free bottoms of sand or mud, particularly when the sea is calm and clear.

Many species hunt by sight under these conditions and movement can be achieved by selecting the right weight of smooth lead, such as an Arlesey bomb, and casting uptide so that the pull of the current rolls the bait round slowly in a wide arc.

When fishing in this manner, remember that the currents will tend to slacken or increase according to the stage of the tide. That's why I always attach my lead with a spring link swivel so the sinker can be easily switched to suit changing conditions.

# RUNNING LEGER TRACE

Another good way to search an area of smooth ground between snags is to cast out with a flat-sided torpedo lead. This will not roll and become snagged like an Arlesey but movement can be obtained by reeling in a turn or two of line every few minutes.

The curiosity of flatfish is often aroused by using a vibrating attractor spoon a few inches above the baited hook. For this type of fishing and for other methods where the bait is best kept hard on the sea bed, I prefer to use a simple running leger tackle.

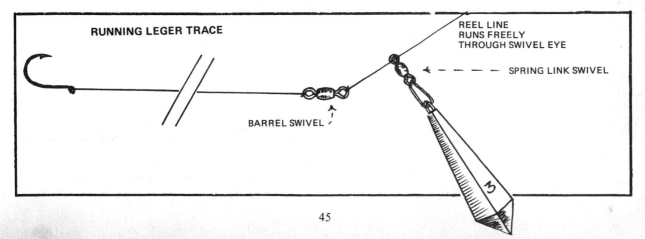

RUNNING LEGER TRACE

REEL LINE RUNS FREELY THROUGH SWIVEL EYE

SPRING LINK SWIVEL

BARREL SWIVEL

# SLIDING FLOAT RIG

There are many situations when fishing a bait off the bottom is more successful. Mackerel, garfish, pollack, coalfish, wrasse and bass frequently seek their food in the upper layers of water.

When the sea is clear, float tackle can provide exciting sport from a high vantage point, such as a pier or deepwater rock ledge. There are few more stimulating sights than a float plunging down abruptly into the depths when a great slabsided pollack hits the bait!

Sliding floats have more application in sea fishing than the fixed variety, as they allow fishing at depths exceeding the length of the rod.

The guiding principle is to employ a float of just sufficient buoyancy to support the bait under prevailing conditions.

If the float is too big many fish will reject the bait because of excess drag.

Hooks should be mounted on wire when hunting such species as conger, tope and dogfish.

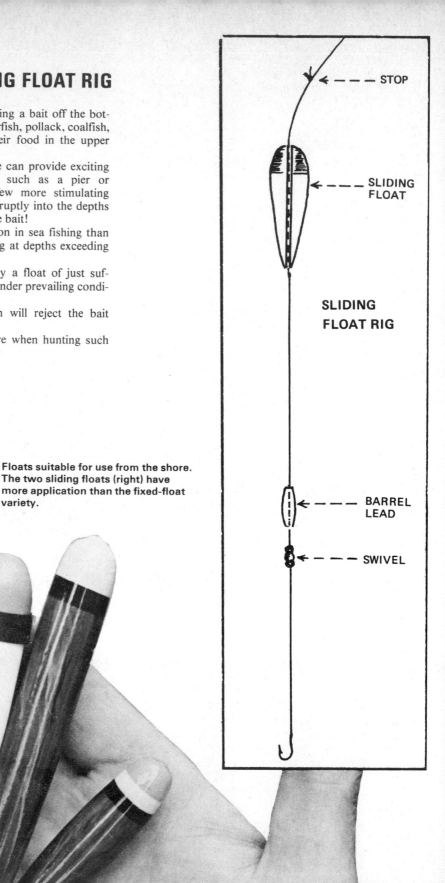

Floats suitable for use from the shore. The two sliding floats (right) have more application than the fixed-float variety.

# reservoir trout fishing

## Spotting the hotspots—

**with**

**DICK SHRIVE**

TROUT anglers who sample half-a-dozen different waters in the course of a fishing year will obviously enjoy themselves and take fish. But they cannot compete with the locals when it comes to results, for the man who gets consistently good returns is usually the man with the greatest store of local knowledge.

The little observations and conclusions made after each trip are stored away—sometimes subconsciously—in the memory until a complete picture of the water is built-up. This accumulation of knowledge stands in good stead when other anglers are not doing so well.

As an example, let me quote what happened at Ravensthorpe—a reservoir I have fished for many years—on an Easter Tuesday. When I and a companion arrived there were already 129 anglers doing their stuff . . . on a water which used to have a limit of six rods!

It was a fairly windy day and, at first, it didn't look as if there was enough space available to squeeze in another angler. But a closer look showed there was a fishable gap in the ranks, smack in the middle of one bank. Unknown to neighbouring anglers that gap was the real hotspot in the prevailing conditions.

The wind blowing square on to one bank had set up a current from each corner, both of which ran along the bank until they converged. Where they met, they changed direction and ran out towards the middle and this strong underflow was where the trout had congregated. Knowing this was where the fish would be, it wasn't difficult to take a limit catch—not by any superior methods but simply by knowing the water.

A good trout in the net for Dick Shrive—the result of knowing exactly where to fish in the water that he visited.

In a strong wind there is always a current coming away from the lee shore. Sometimes, as in the case of a new reservoir, it will be easy to spot because it will make a mud slick in the clear water. But on a mature water, where the bottom is more consolidated or where the current is now too strong, there will be no obvious visual signs—and this is where local knowledge comes in.

My advice to anyone who is bank-fishing a new water for the first time is to fish the lee shore if the wind is blowing. Find the current coming away from the bank, or in some cases, running parallel to it (see diagram) and you will find trout. Don't worry if the current is almost solid with suspended silt and muck. In my experience the trout are not the slightest bit put out by it.

On a calm day the tactics would be different. There are no currents so what I would search for then would be the deepest water I could cover. Trout will come closer inshore on calm days but they do like a drop of water over their heads. But I don't like fishing in too great a depth. Water that is 10 feet to 15 feet deep is always enough for me, even from a boat. I know there is often the odd trout feeding near the bottom in depths of water up to 40 ft. but it's a waste of time trying for them.

An ordinary sinking line of the type I use doesn't usually go down more than about nine feet or so, which leaves 30 feet of water underneath. But a trout in 10 feet of water is quite willing to swim up, say 8 ft. to take your fly. It is very unlikely it will come up from the bottom in 40 ft. The ideal depth is one in which you can comfortably fish both the top strata of water and the bottom at the same time.

A mark off Falmouth, Cornwall, produced this new boat-fishing record haddock of 13 lb. 11¼ oz. for Hailsham angler George Bones in June, 1978.

Pensioner Bert Pike, of Alderney, Channel Islands, entered the national shore records list with this superb 4½ lb. sole, caught from Alderney's Platte Saline beach in November, 1978.

# BRITISH RECORD FISH LIST

*Recognised as at January 1979*

# SEA FISH (Boat Records)

| | lb. | oz. | dr. : | Weight kilo. | grms. | Captor and Venue | Date |
|---|---|---|---|---|---|---|---|
| Angler Fish | 82 | 12 | 0 : | 37 | 533 | K. Ponsford, Mevagissey, Cornwall | 1977 |
| Bass | 18 | 6 | 0 : | 8 | 334 | R. G. Slater, off Eddystone Reef, Plymouth | 1975 |
| Black-fish | 3 | 10 | 8 : | 1 | 658 | James Semple, off Head of Ayr, Scotland | 1972 |
| Bluemouth | 3 | 2 | 8 : | 1 | 431 | Anne Lyneholm, Loch Shell, Stornoway | 1976 |
| Bogue | 1 | 10 | 0 : | 0 | 737 | D. R. Northam, Plymouth | 1975 |
| Bream, Black | 6 | 14 | 4 : | 3 | 118 | J. Garlick (Torquay), Wreck off Devon coast | 1977 |
| Bream, Gilthead | 5 | 0 | 0 : | 2 | 268 | A. H. Stratton-Knott, off St. Mawes, Cornwall | 1978 |
| Bream, Ray's | 6 | 3 | 13 : | 2 | 829 | J. Holland, Barra Head, Scotland | 1978 |
| Bream, Red | 9 | 8 | 12 : | 4 | 330 | B. H. Reynolds, off Mevagissey, Cornwall | 1974 |
| Brill | 16 | 0 | 0 : | 7 | 257 | A. H. Fisher, Isle of Man | 1950 |
| Bull Huss | 21 | 3 | 0 : | 9 | 610 | J. Holmes, Looe, Cornwall | 1955 |
| Catfish | 15 | 12 | 0 : | 7 | 144 | E. Fisher, off Filey, Yorks | 1973 |
| Coalfish | 30 | 12 | 0 : | 13 | 947 | A. F. Harris, Eddystone, Devon | 1973 |
| Cod | 53 | 0 | 0 : | 24 | 039 | G. Martin, Start Point, Devon | 1972 |
| Comber | 1 | 13 | 0 : | 0 | 822 | B. Phillips, Mounts Bay, Cornwall | 1977 |
| Common Skate | 226 | 8 | 0 : | 102 | 733 | R. S. Macpherson, Duny Voe, Shetland | 1970 |
| Conger | 109 | 6 | 0 : | 49 | 607 | R. W. Potter, S.E. of Eddystone, Plymouth | 1976 |
| Dab | 2 | 12 | 4 : | 1 | 254 | R. Islip, Gairloch, Wester Ross, Scotland | 1975 |
| Dogfish, Black-Mouthed | 2 | 13 | 8 : | 1 | 288 | J. H. Anderson, Loch Fyne, Scotland | 1977 |
| Dogfish, Lesser Spotted | 4 | 1 | 13 : | 1 | 863 | B. J. Solomon, Newquay, Cornwall | 1976 |
| Flounder | 5 | 11 | 8 : | 2 | 593 | A. G. L. Cobbledick, Fowey, Cornwall | 1956 |
| Forkbeard, Greater | 4 | 11 | 4 : | 2 | 133 | Miss M. Woodgate, Falmouth Bay, Cornwall | 1969 |

| | Weight | | | | | Captor and Venue | Date |
|---|---|---|---|---|---|---|---|
| | lb. | oz. | dr. : | kilo. | grms. | | |
| Garfish | 2 | 13 | 14 : | 1 | 300 | S. Claeskens, off Newton Ferrers, Devon | 1971 |
| Greater Weever | 2 | 4 | 0 : | 1 | 020 | P. Ainslie, Brighton | 1927 |
| Gurnard, Grey | 2 | 7 | 0 : | 1 | 104 | D. Swinbanks, Caliach Point, Mull, Scotland | 1976 |
| Gurnard, Red | 5 | 0 | 0 : | 2 | 268 | B. D. Critchley, off Rhyl, Wales | 1973 |
| Gurnard, Streaked | 1 | 0 | 0 : | 0 | 454 | Qualifying weight | — |
| Gurnard, Yellow or Tubfish | 11 | 7 | 4 : | 5 | 195 | C. W. King, Wallasey, Cheshire | 1952 |
| Haddock | 13 | 11 | 4 : | 6 | 215 | G. Bones, off Falmouth, Cornwall | 1978 |
| Haddock, Norway | 1 | 13 | 8 : | 0 | 836 | T. Barrett, off Southend | 1975 |
| Hake | 25 | 5 | 8 : | 11 | 494 | H. W. Steele, Belfast Lough, Nth Ireland | 1962 |
| Halibut | 212 | 4 | 0 : | 96 | 270 | J. A. Hewitt, off Dunnet Head, Caithness | 1975 |
| Herring | 1 | 1 | 0 : | 0 | 481 | Brett Barden, off Bexhill, Sussex | 1973 |
| John Dory | 11 | 14 | 0 : | 5 | 386 | J. Johnson, Newhaven, Sussex | 1977 |
| Ling | 57 | 2 | 8 : | 25 | 924 | H. Solomons, off Mevagissey, Cornwall | 1975 |
| Lumpsucker | 6 | 3 | 4 : | 2 | 813 | F. Harrison, Redcar, Yorks | 1968 |
| Mackerel | 5 | 6 | 8 : | 2 | 452 | S. Beasley, Eddystone, Devon | 1969 |
| Megrim | 3 | 12 | 8 : | 1 | 714 | P. Christie, Loch Gairloch, Scotland | 1973 |
| Monkfish | 66 | 0 | 0 : | 29 | 936 | C. G. Chalk, Shoreham, Sussex | 1965 |
| Mullet, Golden Grey | 1 | 9 | 15 : | 0 | 735 | B. R. Morin, off Jersey, C.I. | 1978 |
| Mullet, Red | 3 | 8 | 0 : | 1 | 587 | Qualifying weight | — |
| Mullet, Thick-Lipped Grey | 10 | 1 | 0 : | 4 | 564 | P. C. Libby, Portland, Dorset | 1952 |
| Mullet, Thin-Lipped Grey | 4 | 0 | 0 : | 1 | 814 | Qualifying weight | — |
| Opah | 128 | 0 | Q : | 58 | 057 | A. R. Blewett, Mounts Bay, Penzance | 1973 |
| Pelamid, (Bonito) | 8 | 13 | 4 : | 4 | 004 | J. Parnell, Torbay, Devon | 1969 |
| Perch, Dusky | 28 | 0 | 0 : | 12 | 700 | D. Cope, off Durlston Head, Dorset | 1973 |
| Plaice | 10 | 3 | 8 : | 4 | 624 | H. Gardiner, Longasound, Scotland | 1974 |
| Pollack | 25 | 0 | 0 : | 11 | 339 | R. J. Hosking, Eddystone, Devon | 1972 |
| Pouting (Bib. Pout) | 5 | 8 | 0 : | 2 | 494 | R. S. Armstrong, off Berry Head, Devon | 1969 |
| Ray, Blonde | 37 | 12 | 0 : | 17 | 122 | H. T. Pout, off Start Point, Devon | 1973 |
| Ray, Bottle-nosed | 76 | 0 | 0 : | 34 | 471 | R. Bulpitt, off Needles, Isle of Wight | 1970 |
| Ray, Cuckoo | 5 | 11 | 0 : | 2 | 579 | V. Morrison, off Causeway Coast, N.I. | 1975 |
| Ray, Eagle | 52 | 8 | 0 : | 23 | 812 | R. J. Smith, off Nab Tower, Isle of Wight | 1972 |
| Ray, Electric | 96 | 1 | 0 : | 43 | 571 | N. J. Cowley, off Dodman Point, Cornwall | 1975 |
| Ray, Sandy | 4 | 0 | 0 : | 1 | 814 | Qualifying weight | — |
| Ray, Small-eyed | 16 | 4 | 0 : | 7 | 370 | H. T. Pout, Salcombe, Devon | 1973 |
| Ray, Spotted | 6 | 3 | 4 : | 2 | 813 | P. J. England, Isle of Mull | 1977 |
| Ray, Sting | 59 | 0 | 0 : | 26 | 761 | J. M. Buckley, Clacton, Essex | 1952 |
| Ray, Thornback | 38 | 0 | 0 : | 17 | 236 | J. Patterson, Rustington, Sussex | 1935 |
| Ray, Undulate | 19 | 6 | 13 : | 8 | 811 | L. R. Le Page, Herm, Channel Islands | 1970 |
| Rockling, 3-bearded | 3 | 2 | 0 : | 1 | 424 | N. Docksey, Portland Breakwater, Dorset | 1976 |
| Rockling, Shore | 1 | 0 | 0 : | 0 | 454 | Qualifying weight | — |
| Salmon, Coho | | | | | | Minimum qualifying weight to be finalised | |
| Sea-scorpion, Short-spinned | 2 | 3 | 0 : | 0 | 992 | R. Stephenson, Gt. Cumbrae Island, Scotland | 1976 |
| Scad (Horse Mackerel) | 3 | 5 | 3 : | 1 | 507 | M. A. Atkins, Torbay, Devon | 1978 |
| Shad, Allis | 3 | 0 | 0 : | 1 | 361 | Qualifying weight | — |
| Shad, Twaite | (3 | 2 | 0 : | 1 | 417) | T. Hayward, Deal | 1949 |
| | (3 | 2 | 0 : | 1 | 417) | S. Jenkins, Torbay | 1954 |
| Shark, Blue | 218 | 0 | 0 : | 98 | 878 | N. Sutcliffe, Looe, Cornwall | 1959 |
| Shark, Mako | 500 | 0 | 0 : | 226 | 786 | Mrs. J. M. Yallop, off Eddystone, Devon | 1971 |
| Shark, Porbeagle | 465 | 0 | 0 : | 210 | 911 | J. Potier, off Padstow, Cornwall | 1976 |
| Shark, Thresher | 295 | 0 | 0 : | 133 | 804 | H. J. Aris, Dunose Head, I.o.W. | 1978 |
| Shark, Six Gilled | 9 | 8 | 0 : | 4 | 308 | F. E. Beeton, Penlee Point, Plymouth | 1976 |
| Smoothhound, Starry | 20 | 15 | 12 : | 9 | 520 | B. J. Allpress, Bradwell-on-Sea, Essex | 1978 |
| Smoothhound | 28 | 0 | 0 : | 12 | 700 | A. T. Chilvers, Heacham, Norfolk | 1969 |
| Sole | 4 | 0 | 0 : | 1 | 814 | Qualifying weight | — |
| Sole, Lemon | 2 | 2 | 0 : | 0 | 963 | J. Gordon, Loch Goil Head, Scotland | 1976 |
| Spanish Mackerel | 1 | 0 | 6 : | 0 | 464 | P. Jones, off Guernsey, C.I. | 1972 |
| Spurdog | 21 | 3 | 7 : | 9 | 624 | P. Barrett, Porthleven, Cornwall | 1977 |
| Sunfish | 108 | 0 | 0 : | 48 | 986 | T. F. Sisson, Saundersfoot, Pembs., Wales | 1976 |
| Tadpole fish | 1 | 0 | 0 : | 0 | 454 | Qualifying weight | — |
| Tope | 74 | 11 | 0 : | 33 | 876 | A. B. Harries, Caldy Island | .1964 |
| Torsk | 12 | 1 | 0 : | 5 | 471 | D. Pottinger, Shetland | 1968 |
| Trigger Fish | 4 | 9 | 5 : | 2 | 077 | E. Montacute, Weymouth | 1975 |
| Tunny | 851 | 0 | 0 : | 385 | 989 | L. Mitchell Henry, Whitby, Yorks | 1933 |
| Turbot | 32 | 3 | 0 : | 14 | 599 | D. Dyer, off Plymouth, Devon | 1976 |
| Witch | 1 | 0 | 0 : | 0 | 454 | Qualifying weight | — |
| Whiting | 6 | 4 | 0 : | 2 | 834 | S. Dearman, West Bay, Bridport, Dorset | 1977 |
| Whiting, Blue (Poutassou) | 1 | 12 | 0 : | 0 | 793 | J. H. Anderson, Loch Fyne, Scotland | 1977 |
| Wrasse, Ballan | 7 | 8 | 5 : | 3 | 409 | M. B. Hale, North of Herm, Channel Islands | 1975 |
| Wrasse, Cuckoo | 2 | 0 | 8 : | 0 | 921 | A. M. Foley, off Plymouth | 1973 |
| Wreck Fish | 7 | 10 | 0 : | 3 | 458 | Commander E. St. John Holt, off Looe, Cornwall | 1974 |

# SEA FISH (Shore Records)

| | | | | | | | |
|---|---|---|---|---|---|---|---|
| Angler Fish | 68 | 2 | 0 : | 30 | 899 | J. G. T. Legerton, Canvey Island, Essex | 1967 |
| Bass | 18 | 2 | 0 : | 8 | 220 | F. C. Borley, Felixstowe, Suffolk | 1943 |
| Black-fish | 2 | 0 | 0 : | 0 | 907 | Qualifying weight | — |
| Bluemouth | 2 | 0 | 0 : | 0 | 907 | Qualifying weight | — |

| | Weight | | | | | Captor and Venue | Date |
|---|---|---|---|---|---|---|---|
| | lb. | oz. | dr. : | kilo. | grms. | | |
| Bogue | 1 | 15 | 4 : | 0 | 885 | S. G. Torode, Pembroke, Guernsey, C.I. | 1978 |
| Bream, Black | 4 | 14 | 4 : | 2 | 217 | R. J. Holloway, Admiralty Pier, Dover | 1977 |
| Bream, Gilthead | 6 | 15 | 0 : | 3 | 146 | H. Solomons, Salcombe Estuary, Devon | 1977 |
| Bream, Ray's | 7 | 15 | 12 : | 3 | 621 | G. Walker, Crimdon Beach, Hartlepool | 1967 |
| Bream, Red | 3 | 0 | 0 : | 1 | 361 | D. J. Berry, Alderney, C.I. | 1976 |
| Brill | 5 | 12 | 4 : | 2 | 615 | M. Freeman, Chesil Beach, Dorset | 1976 |
| Bull Huss | 17 | 15 | 0 : | 8 | 135 | M. Roberts, Falmouth | 1977 |
| Catfish | 12 | 12 | 8 : | 5 | 797 | G. M. Taylor, Stonehaven, Scotland | 1978 |
| Coalfish | 16 | 8 | 8 : | 7 | 498 | N. Randall, Plymouth | 1977 |
| Cod | 44 | 8 | 0 : | 20 | 183 | B. Jones, Toms Points, Barry, Glam. | 1966 |
| Comber | 1 | 0 | 0 : | 0 | 454 | Qualifying weight | — |
| Common Skate | 150 | 0 | 0 : | 68 | 036 | Qualifying weight | — |
| Conger | 67 | 1 | 0 : | 30 | 418 | A. W. Lander, Arch Rock End, Torquay | 1977 |
| Dab | 2 | 9 | 8 : | 1 | 176 | M. L. Watts, Port Talbot, Wales | 1936 |
| Dogfish, Black-Mouthed | 1 | 0 | 0 : | 0 | 454 | Qualifying weight | — |
| Dogfish, Lesser Spotted | 4 | 8 | 0 : | 2 | 040 | J. Beattie, off Ayr Pier, Scotland | 1969 |
| Flounder | 4 | 7 | 0 : | 2 | 012 | M. King, Seaford Beach, Newhaven | 1976 |
| Forkbeard, Greater | 2 | 0 | 0 : | 0 | 907 | Qualifying weight | — |
| Garfish | 2 | 8 | 0 : | 1 | 134 | S. Lester, Pembroke, Guernsey, C.I. | 1977 |
| Greater Weever | 2 | 0 | 0 : | 0 | 907 | Qualifying weight | — |
| Gurnard, Grey | 1 | 8 | 0 : | 0 | 680 | S. Quine, Isle of Man | 1977 |
| Gurnard, Red | 2 | 10 | 11 : | 1 | 435 | D. Johns, Helford River, Cornwall | 1976 |
| Gurnard, Streaked | 1 | 6 | 8 : | 0 | 637 | H. Livingstone Smith, Loch Goil, Firth of Clyde | 1971 |
| Gurnard, Yellow or Tubfish | 12 | 3 | 0 : | 5 | 527 | G. J. Reynolds, Langland Bay, Wales | 1976 |
| Haddock | 6 | 12 | 0 : | 3 | 061 | G. B. Stevenson, Loch Goil, Firth of Clyde | 1976 |
| Haddock, Norway | 1 | 3 | 0 : | 0 | 538 | F. P. Fawke, Southend Pier, Essex | 1973 |
| Hake | 5 | 0 | 0 : | 2 | 268 | Qualifying weight | — |
| Halibut | 14 | 0 | 0 : | 6 | 350 | Qualifying weight | — |
| Herring | 1 | 0 | 0 : | 0 | 454 | Qualifying weight | — |
| John Dory | 4 | 0 | 0 : | 1 | 814 | Qualifying weight | — |
| Ling | 15 | 5 | 11 : | 6 | 965 | P. Sanders, Porthleven Beach, Cornwall | 1976 |
| Lumpsucker | 14 | 3 | 0 : | 6 | 435 | W. J. Burgess, off Felixstowe Beach, Suffolk | 1970 |
| Mackerel | 4 | 0 | 8 : | 1 | 828 | P. Porter, Breakwater, Peel, Isle of Man | 1952 |
| Megrim | 2 | 0 | 0 : | 0 | 907 | Qualifying weight | — |
| Monkfish | 50 | 0 | 0 : | 22 | 679 | Qualifying weight | — |
| Mullet, Golden Grey | 2 | 10 | 0 : | 1 | 190 | R. J. Hopkins, Burry Port, Llanelli, Wales | 1976 |
| Mullet, Red | 3 | 10 | 0 : | 1 | 644 | J. E. Martell, Guernsey, C.I. | 1967 |
| Mullet, Thick-Lipped Grey | 10 | 0 | 12 : | 4 | 557 | R. Gifford, Lagoon Leys, Aberthaw, Glam. | 1978 |
| Mullet, Thin-Lipped Grey | 5 | 11 | 0 : | 2 | 579 | D. E. Knowles, River Rother, Sussex | 1975 |
| Opah | 40 | 0 | 0 : | 18 | 143 | Qualifying weight | — |
| Pelamid (Bonito) | 4 | 0 | 0 : | 1 | 814 | Qualifying weight | — |
| Perch, Dusky | 14 | 0 | 0 : | 6 | 350 | Qualifying weight | — |
| Plaice | 8 | 1 | 4 : | 3 | 663 | N. Mills, Southend Pier | 1976 |
| Pollack | 16 | 0 | 0 : | 7 | 257 | B. Raybould, Portland Bill, Dorset | 1977 |
| Pouting (Bib, Pout) | 3 | 4 | 0 : | 1 | 474 | P. T. Weekes, Dover Breakwater | 1978 |
| Ray, Blonde | 25 | 4 | 0 : | 11 | 452 | S. B. Sangan, Greve De Lecq Pier, Jersey, C.I. | 1975 |
| Ray, Bottle-nosed | 30 | 0 | 0 : | 13 | 607 | Qualifying weight | — |
| Ray, Cuckoo | 4 | 8 | 0 : | 2 | 040 | Qualifying weight | — |
| Ray, Eagle | 25 | 0 | 0 : | 11 | 339 | Qualifying weight | — |
| Ray, Electric | 47 | 8 | 0 : | 21 | 544 | R. J. F. Pearce, Long Quarry, Torquay, Devon | 1971 |
| Ray, Sandy | 4 | 0 | 0 : | 1 | 814 | Qualifying weight | — |
| Ray, Small-eyed | 13 | 8 | 15 : | 6 | 149 | A. Jones, Trevose Head, Cornwall | 1976 |
| Ray, Spotted | 7 | 12 | 0 : | 3 | 514 | P. Dower, Plymouth | 1977 |
| Ray, Sting | 51 | 4 | 0 : | 23 | 245 | A. L. Stevens, Sowley Beach, Hants | 1975 |
| Ray, Thornback | 19 | 0 | 0 : | 8 | 618 | A. K. Paterson, Mull of Galloway, Scotland | 1976 |
| Ray, Undulate | 10 | 10 | 4 : | 4 | 826 | G. S. Robert, Port Soif Bay, Guernsey, C.I. | 1968 |
| Rockling, 3-bearded | 2 | 14 | 8 : | 1 | 317 | N. S. Burt, Portland, Dorset | 1976 |
| Rockling, Shore | 1 | 1 | 4 : | 0 | 488 | A. Bayes, Gristhorpe, Scarborough | 1976 |
| Salmon, Coho | 1 | 8 | 1 : | 0 | 681 | R. J. McCracken, St. Sampsons, Guernsey, C.I. | 1977 |
| Sea Scorpion (Short-spined) | 2 | 2 | 8 : | 0 | 977 | R. W. Tarn, Roker South Pier, Sunderland | 1972 |
| Scad (Horse Mackerel) | 2 | 5 | 13 : | 1 | 162 | W. Rail, North Cliffs, Cornwall | 1977 |
| Shad, Allis | 4 | 12 | 7 : | 2 | 168 | P. Gerrard, Chesil Beach, Dorset | 1977 |
| Shad, Twaite | 2 | 12 | 0 | 1 | 247 | J. W. Martin, Garlieston, Wigtownshire, Scotland | 1978 |
| Shark, Blue | 75 | 0 | 0 : | 34 | 018 | Qualifying weight | — |
| Shark, Mako | 75 | 0 | 0 : | 34 | 018 | Qualifying weight | — |
| Shark, Porbeagle | 75 | 0 | 0 : | 34 | 018 | Qualifying weight | — |
| Shark, Thresher | 75 | 0 | 0 : | 34 | 018 | Qualifying weight | — |
| Smoothhound, Starry | 23 | 2 | 0 : | 10 | 488 | D. Carpenter, Beach, Bradwell-on-Sea, Essex | 1972 |
| Smoothhound | 14 | 14 | 12 : | 6 | 767 | A. Peacock, St. Donats, Glam. | 1977 |
| Sole | 4 | 8 | 0 : | 2 | 041 | H. C. L. Pike, Platte Saline Beach, Alderney, C.I. | 1978 |
| Sole, Lemon | 2 | 2 | 15 : | 0 | 990 | D. R. Duke, Victoria Pier, Douglas, Isle of Man | 1971 |
| Spanish Mackerel | 1 | 0 | 0 : | 0 | 454 | Qualifying weight | — |
| Spurdog | 16 | 12 | 8 : | 7 | 611 | R. Legg, Chesil Beach, Dorset | 1964 |
| Sunfish | 49 | 4 | 0 : | 22 | 338 | M. Merry, North Cliffs, Cornwall | 1976 |
| Tadpole Fish | 1 | 3 | 12 : | 0 | 595 | D. Higgins, Whitley Bay, Tyne and Wear | 1977 |
| Tope | 54 | 4 | 0 : | 24 | 606 | D. Hastings, Loch Ryan, Wigtownshire, Scotland | 1975 |
| Torsk | 5 | 0 | 0 : | 2 | 268 | Qualifying weight | — |
| Trigger Fish | 4 | 6 | 0 : | 1 | 984 | M. J. Blew, Bossington Beach, Somerset | 1975 |
| Tunny | 100 | 0 | 0 : | 45 | 357 | Qualifying weight | — |
| Turbot | 28 | 8 | 0 : | 12 | 926 | J. D. Dorling, Dunwich Beach, Suffolk | 1973 |
| Witch | 1 | 2 | 13 : | 0 | 533 | T. J. Barathy, Colwyn Bay, Wales | 1967 |
| Whiting | 3 | 2 | 0 : | 1 | 417 | C. T. Kochevar, Dungeness | 1976 |
| Wrasse, Ballan | 8 | 6 | 6 : | 3 | 808 | R. W. LePage, Bordeaux Beach, Guernsey, C.I. | 1976 |
| Wrasse, Cuckoo | 1 | 4 | 8 : | 0 | 581 | R. Newton, Holyhead Breakwater, Wales | 1973 |
| Wreck Fish | 2 | 0 | 0 : | 0 | 907 | Qualifying weight | — |

# Mini sea records —Weights up to 1 lb.

## SPECIES

| | Weight | | | Captor and Venue | Date |
|---|---|---|---|---|---|
| | oz. | dr. | : grms. | | |
| Argentine | 5 | 3 | : 147 | I. Millar, Loch Long, Scotland | 1978 |
| Blenny, Tompot | 5 | 2 | : 144 | J. Hughes, Portland Bill, Dorset | 1977 |
| Blenny, Viviparous | 11 | 3 | : 317 | D. Ramsey, Craigendoran, Scotland | 1975 |
| Dab, Long Rough | 5 | 8 | : 155 | I. McGrath, Coulport, Loch Long, Scotland | 1975 |
| Dragonet | 5 | 5 | : 150 | T. J. Carter, off Hastings | 1978 |
| Goby, Black | 1 | 8 | : 042 | P. J. Whippy, from Pevensey Bay, Sussex | 1975 |
| Goby, Giant | 6 | 10 | : 187 | P. A. Cadogan, Herm Is., Nr Guernsey, C.I. | 1974 |
| Goby, Rock | 0 | 14 | : 024 | C. L. Phillips, Menai Straits, Wales | 1977 |
| Pilchard | 7 | 0 | : 198 | K. W. Jarrett, Littlehampton, Sussex | 1976 |
| Poor Cod | 10 | 5 | : 294 | H. Livingstone Smith, Gantocks, Scotland | 1976 |
| Red Band Fish | 13 | 8 | : 382 | K. Bradbury, off Paignton, Devon | 1975 |
| Rockling, Five-Bearded | 9 | 4 | : 262 | P. R. Winder, Lancing Beach, Sussex | 1968 |
| Sandeel, Corbin's | 4 | 6 | : 124 | M. J. Priaulx, off Plymouth | 1975 |
| Sandeel, Greater | 7 | 12 | : 219 | P. Lucas, Herm, Channel Islands | 1977 |
| Sea Scorpion (Long-spined) | 8 | 0 | : 226 | W. Crone, Plymouth | 1978 |
| Shanny | 2 | 5 | : 66 | K. Woolfe, Guernsey | 1977 |
| Smelt | 5 | 9 | : 158 | B. Wyganowski, Southend Pier | 1978 |
| Smelt, Sand | 2 | 9 | : 072 | A. D. Laws, St. Peter Port, Guernsey, C.I. | 1975 |
| Stickleback, Sea | 0 | 4 | : 007 | K. Pilley, Poole Harbour, Dorset | 1978 |
| Topknot, Common | 11 | 2 | : 315 | P. Andrews, St. Catherines, Jersey, C.I. | 1972 |
| Weever, Lesser | 2 | 2 | : 060 | M. Nickolls, Schole Bank, off Guernsey, C.I. | 1976 |
| Wrasse, Corkwing | 11 | 4 | : 318 | T. R. Woodman, off Portland Bill, Dorset | 1974 |
| Wrasse, Goldsinny | 2 | 9 | : 072 | R. Lambert, Portland Bill, Dorset | 1977 |
| Wrasse, Rock Cook | 2 | 9 | : 072 | A. L. C. de Guerin, St. Peter Port, C.I. | 1977 |

Londoner Barney Allpress (below) helps display the record starry smoothhound of 20 lb. 15 oz. 12 dms., that he caught off Bradwell, Essex, in September, 1978, to fill the vacant title. A minimum qualifying weight of 20 lb. had been set by the Records Committee, so Barney had close on 1 lb. to spare. ▼

Stephen Terry, of West Wittering, Sussex (above) smashed the freshwater eel record with this monster of 11 lb. 2 oz., taken from Kingfisher Lake, near Ringwood, Hants.

# FRESHWATER FISH

| | lb. | oz. | dr. : | kilo. | grms. | Captor and Venue | Date |
|---|---|---|---|---|---|---|---|
| Barbel | 13 | 12 | 0 : | 6 | 237 | J. Day, Hampshire Avon | 1962 |
| Bleak | 0 | 3 | 15 : | 0 | 111 | D. Pollard, Staythorpe Pond, nr Newark, Notts | 1971 |
| Bream (Common, Bronze) | 13 | 8 | 0 : | 6 | 123 | A. R. Heslop, private water in Staffordshire | 1977 |
| Bullhead (Miller's Thumb) | 0 | 0 | 10 : | 0 | 017 | E. Harrison, Leeds & Liverpool Canal | 1978 |
| *Carp | 44 | 0 | 0 : | 19 | 957 | R. Walker, Redmire Pool | 1952 |
| Carp, Crucian | 5 | 10 | 8 : | 2 | 565 | G. Halls, Lakes, Kings Lynn, Norfolk | 1976 |
| Catfish (Wels) | 43 | 8 | 0 : | 19 | 730 | R. J. Bray, Wilstone Reservoir, Tring, Herts | 1970 |
| Char | 1 | 12 | 4 : | 0 | 801 | C. Imperiale, Loch Insh, Inverness-shire | 1974 |
| Chub | 7 | 6 | 0 : | 3 | 345 | W. L. Warren, Hampshire Avon | 1957 |
| Dace | 1 | 4 | 4 : | 0 | 574 | J. L. Gasson, Little Ouse, Thetford, Norfolk | 1960 |
| Eel | 11 | 2 | 0 : | 5 | 046 | S. Terry, Kingfisher Lake, Nr. Ringwood, Hants | 1978 |
| Gudgeon | 0 | 4 | 4 : | 0 | 123 | M. Bowen, pond at Ebbw Vale | 1977 |
| Gwyniad (Whitefish) | 1 | 4 | 0 : | 0 | 567 | J. R. Williams, Llyn Tegid, Wales | 1965 |
| Loch Lomond Powan | 1 | 7 | 0 : | 0 | 652 | J. M. Ryder, Loch Lomond, Scotland | 1972 |
| Minnow | 0 | 0 | 9 : | 0 | 016 | R. Guy, River Rother, Midhurst, Sussex | 1978 |
| Orfe, Golden | 4 | 3 | 0 : | 1 | 899 | B. T. Mills, River Test, Hampshire | 1976 |
| Perch | 4 | 12 | 0 : | 2 | 154 | S. F. Baker, Oulton Broad | 1962 |
| Pike | 40 | 0 | 0 : | 18 | 143 | P. D. Hancock, Horsey Mere, Norfolk | 1967 |
| Pike-perch (Walleye) | 11 | 12 | 0 : | 5 | 329 | F. Adams, Delph, Welney, Cambs | 1934 |
| Pike-perch (Zander) | 17 | 4 | 0 : | 7 | 828 | D. Litton, Gt. Ouse, Relief Channel | 1977 |
| Pumpkinseed | 0 | 2 | 10 : | 0 | 074 | A. Baverstock, GLC Highgate Pond, London | 1977 |
| Roach | 4 | 1 | 0 : | 1 | 842 | R. G. Jones, Notts. gravel pit | 1975 |
| *Rudd | 4 | 8 | 0 : | 2 | 041 | Rev. E. C. Alston, Thetford, Norfolk | 1933 |
| Ruffe | 0 | 5 | 0 : | 0 | 141 | P. Barrowcliffe, Bure, Norfolk | 1977 |
| *Salmon | 64 | 0 | 0 : | 29 | 029 | Miss G. W. Ballantyne, River Tay, Scotland | 1922 |
| Schelly (Skelly) | 1 | 10 | 0 : | 0 | 737 | W. Wainwright, Ullswater, Cumbria | 1976 |
| Tench | 10 | 1 | 2 : | 5 | 567 | L. W. Brown, Peterborough, Brick Pit | 1975 |
| Trout, American Brook (Brook Charr) | 4 | 8 | 8 : | 2 | 055 | A. Pearson, Avington Fishery, Hants | 1978 |
| Trout, Brown | 19 | 9 | 4 : | 8 | 880 | A. Jackson, Loch Quoish, Inverness-shire | 1978 |
| Trout, Rainbow | 19 | 8 | 0 : | 8 | 844 | A. Pearson, Avington Fishery, Hants | 1977 |

\* Denotes fish for which the cast or body was available for inspection: Caught before the formation of the Committee.

Species open for freshwater fish claims (Minimum qualifying weights). **Grayling** (3 lb.); **Sea Trout** (20 lb.); **Silver Bream** (1½ lb.). Qualifying weights are subject to revision by the Committee if necessary.

☐ The Editor wishes to thank Mr. Peter Tombleson and the British Record (rod-caught) Fish Committee for their assistance in compiling these lists.

# HAVE YOU HOOKED A RECORD?

EVERY angler dreams of landing a record but those dreams could quickly turn into a nightmare of disappointment if a few, but most important, basic rules of claim are not followed. The British Record (rod-caught) Fish Committee is fair but firm and their stringent safeguards aim to protect the integrity of record status.

First, contact the Committee Secretary (address and telephone number shown below) for advice on preservation, identification and correct claims procedure. He wants the claim in writing, stating species, weight, date and place of capture, tackle used, whether caught from shore or boat (sea fish records are listed in separate sections), plus the names and addresses of reliable independent witnesses of the weight and capture. Witnesses will be required to sign forms supporting the claim, so don't let them get away! In cases where no witnesses are around, a claim can be verified by submitting an affidavit.

But if the Committee is not satisfied about the identification of the species, the way in which it was caught or its weight—no chance.

Correct identification is vital. So keep the fish because no claim will be even considered unless the fish—in its natural state, dead or alive—is available for inspection. The Secretary can advise on producing the fish for examination by a person acting for the Committee.

Medium-sized fish can be kept in a freezer or immersed in formalin solution. If you send by post or rail the fish should be immersed in a solution of one tablespoon of formalin to a pint of water (40 per cent strength). Wrap the fish in a cloth wrung out in the solution, place in a sealed plastic bag and wrap the lot in strong, brown paper. Don't forget to enclose name and address and if the fish is to be returned to you, say so and enclose postage to cover. Weigh the fish before placing in preserving liquids.

Fair angling with rod and line is the golden rule. The Committee defines this as the fish taking a baited hook or lure into its mouth. But the hook or lure must be of a legally-accepted variety and the fish must be played by one person only. Some help is allowed for landing the fish, such as gaffing or netting, but the helper must not touch any part of the tackle other than the leader.

Boat anglers should note that fish caught at sea will be eligible for consideration as records if the boat used sets out from a port in England, Wales, Scotland, Northern Ireland, Isle of Man or Channel Islands and returns to same port without calling at any port outside the United Kingdom. Fish caught in the territorial waters of other countries are not eligible.

Shore fishing is defined as fishing from any land mass or fixed man-made structure. If in doubt, the Committee will always classify the claim on the basis of information supplied.

Fish must be weighed on land, using scales or steelyards which can be tested for accuracy on behalf of the Committee. If possible, use trade or commercial scales that are tested regularly by the Weights and Measures Department. A Weights and Measures Certificate must be produced certifying the accuracy of the scales used and indicating testing at claimed weight. Fish weighing less than a pound must be submitted in grammes.

Fish caught out of season cannot be accepted as new records. And fish suffering from any disease which could enhance the weight are excluded. Burbot are also excluded for conservation reasons.

If you strike lucky, tell ANGLER'S MAIL Newsdesk immediately and let the News Editor know where you are and if photographs are available—or if the fish can be photographed by his photographer. Reverse the charges and follow up with a letter confirming all the details. Newsdesk telephone numbers (01) 261 6025/5980/6016. Address: News Editor, Angler's Mail, King's Reach Tower, Stamford Street, London SE1 9LS.

The Secretary of the British Record (rod-caught) Fish Committee is Mr. Peter Tombleson, National Angler's Council, 5 Cowgate, Peterborough. Telephone: Peterborough (0733) 54084 (day) or 252428 (evening).

# KEEPING AN

**Barrie Rickards has caught hundreds of tench, including more than 60 five-pounders. His best catch is 27 tench (plus three bream) totalling 162 lb. in a single early-morning session. The average weight of the tench was $5\frac{1}{4}$ lb. and the smallest was $4\frac{1}{2}$ lb. No less than 23 of the tench topped the 5 lb. mark.**

Barrie Rickards with part of his best catch of 27 tench, including 23 over 5 lb., all taken on slow-sinking lobworm baits or crust.

TENCH anglers seldom get the chance for direct observations of their quarry—hence the years of debate about where the tench bubbles come from. So this description of tench behaviour is based on my own observations.

We usually fish "blind" for tench, as these fish do not commonly surface-feed and the time of day almost always means the water is too dark to see into it. All the angler sees are clouds of bubbles or the occasional rolling tench. Then, as the light comes up, some cruising fish can be observed.

I used to watch these on Carlton Towers in the West Riding, but after a great deal of observation it became clear that the cruisers were fish which had stopped hard feeding and were wandering about aimlessly.

Occasionally, a tench would take a slow-sinking bait and, just as occasionally, another would dive to the bottom and send up a cloud of bubbles. Tench that indulge in the last trick are probably smelling a likely bloodworm holding a bit of bottom as they swim over it and then dive to investigate for, as I shall show, their eyesight is none too good.

Those cruisers are probably just finishing off the morning feeding stint and as the sun really gets up they depart, either to lurk near the bottom (?) or sunbathe in the lilies. General activity seems to cease until the evening approaches.

In one northern water that I fish the

# EYE ON TENCH

## BARRIE RICKARDS

tench can be observed feeding, simply because they often continue to do so even with a strong sun on their backs. The usual pattern is for the fish to come on feed at about 6 a.m. Naturally, at this time I can see nothing at all except for needle bubbles on the surface. But as it gets lighter and the sun comes up strongly, not only do the tench stop bubbling, but I can see what they are doing down there.

First they cruise either singly or, less commonly, in twos and threes. They creep quietly into the swim and just as quietly leave it again, often to reappear within a few minutes. But this isn't the typical aimless, long cruising of mid-day tench, but short 10-20 yard efforts, interspersed with a good all-heads-down feeding stint.

It is a fascinating sight. In the first place, possibly because the water was still rather cold (June 5, Yorkshire season) they avoided the shadows cast by trees. In late June and July the tench usually stay in the shadows, but here they were enjoying the early season sun. Time and again I saw them wander aimlessly into a shadow and then back-pedal hurriedly to get into the sun.

These small groups of fish got their heads down regularly but they sent up no bubbles at all, so one cannot help but feel that when they are bubbling they really have their heads on the bottom.

The way I had baited up the swim produced interesting behaviour in the tench. They liked the sunlight but avoided like the plague those small areas of bottom, about six inches across, that were covered in white groundbait. In the early morning they undoubtedly mopped up this groundbait but now they were wary of it and concentrated only on the little piles of maggots. Each pile of maggots was about six inches across and consisted of 10-50 maggots dropped by swimfeeder. They could be seen quite clearly, which indicates the clarity of the water and the light conditions.

The tench fed avidly as soon as they chanced upon one of the piles of maggots. I say "chanced" for it was clear to me that although I could see the maggots from the bankside, the tench couldn't see them (or smell them) unless they were within six inches of the outer fringe of each pile. If they wandered past, within those six inches, they immediately turned and devoured every maggot in about 10 seconds flat. If they swam past 12 inches away then they were simply unaware of the maggots.

This behaviour astonished me but fully justified the use of swimfeeders for tench. It may be that at dawn there were many more tench in the swim than I saw later in the mornings and that they scoured the bottom more thoroughly. But if this is not so then scattering groundbait widely and liberally throughout the swim is probably a waste of time—or, at least, a not very efficient way of leading the tench to the hook.

One final point about the "10-second vacuum cleaner". I would see the maggots quite clearly, unless they were obscured by a little puff of mud in front of the tench's nose, but all that happened was that the fish's head waved gently over the patch of maggots and they were all cleaned up very efficiently.

A bite would not register until the tench swam on a little, or unless a very sensitive bite indicating system such as the lift method was in use.

But let's recap on my earlier comments, when I spoke of trying to pin down the aimless wandering of tench into some kind of feeding pattern, and I said early-morning feeders may crowd into optimum feeding areas in large numbers and search intensively for food.

At a later time, around sun-up and after, they go on short walk-abouts, getting their heads down every few minutes. Later still, around mid-day, they go on longer journeys and feed but rarely. After that they take it easy until the evening spell.

If we extend those periods we have to think about evening fishing and night fishing. Having tried tenching at all times, over a wide area of the country, I can never understand the prevarication on the subject—early morning tench fishing is far and away better than at any other time.

I know a Yorkshire lake where the evening fishing is unusually good and at Carlton Towers I did well during the night when September daytime fishing produced almost nothing. Other lakes—usually deep gravel pits in my own experience—can be excellent during the day, but by and large, tench make a habit of feeding in the early morning.

I've already said it is usually impossible to see tench actually feeding at this time, simply because the light is insufficient to light up the bottom for the bank angler. But in some of the very clear Irish loughs the boat fisherman can peer over the side, and, in the reflection of the boat which makes a window into the water, often see a great deal even down to a depth of nine or ten feet.

In my opinion the best feeding period in the early morning is not the "crack of dawn" that we hear so much about, but usually rather later. On many waters this may be around 5.30 a.m. until 7.30 a.m. This is particularly noticeable on the Irish loughs where the tench may feed in the same swims as bream. But the bream feed earlier, most spectacularly just before dawn and for an hour afterwards, and the tench only after they have gone.

Of course, these are generalisations but in my biggest catch the three bream (each over 6 lb.) came right at dawn, then there was a long gap before the first of the 27 big tench. Such feeding orders are also typical of many English waters.

On Lanbeach Lakes, near Cambridge, I used to get bream averaging 4½ lb. in the first 25 minutes of daylight before the tench showed up in the swim. The bream came in from the open water, fed briefly, then left again for the open water. The tench followed, usually arriving rather surreptitiously and in the Irish loughs, at least, I think they came out of reed beds, and in English lakes out of soft weedbeds.

I say "think" because although I've watched them retreat into the reeds once the feeding period is over, I've never actually seen them swim out of the reeds at 5.30 a.m. Nor have I been able to find them in the reeds during the day, even though I've searched carefully. So all the problems are not yet solved.

Peering over the side of a boat with flake clearly visible on the bottom, I am usually aware of tench as I can see a large shape blot out the sight of flake. Trouble is, I've never noticed from which direction they came. Much quieter beasts they are than bream, and the first I knew of their presence was either the shape appearing or a roll of a tench at the surface.

I've never actually seen these tench creating bubbles. They first work about the swim at various depths, in a crowd but not as a shoal. In other words, each tench seems to be an individual following its own path, unlike bream in the same swim, which I've seen only rarely.

It's exciting to see a tench approach the flake. The nose comes up to the bait and it simply disappears in a flash. You can strike at this point but often they blow the bait out again very rapidly. Great fun, whether you hit or miss!

There is a distinct difference between the tench swimming over your bait having decided not to have a go— and the occasion when the flake disappears not under the tench's body but into its mouth.

In the last case the bait vanishes, is sucked in, a split second before the nose of the tench reaches is. In fact, reminiscent of the magggot-mopping tench that I described earlier.

The actual observations I made on the Irish loughs must have been at the equivalent part of the feeding stint to those northern tench, for I never saw them bubbling. The bubbling always preceded the light conditions when I was actually able to watch the fish. In other words, they were beginning to roam.

They show up sporadically in the same swims in the evening but never with a vengeance until the following morning. So tench movements are a bit of a mystery in many ways until we are able to see a lot more of their behaviour from hour to hour.

Mrs. Christine Rickards poses with a 5 lb.-plus tench . . . one of the specimens taken by her husband in early-morning sessions.

A view to brighten the eye of any shore-fishing enthusiast. This deepwater rock mark is on the Irish coast, near Tramore . . . home of big bass, rays, pollack and all kinds of flatfish. But hardly anyone fishes here, reports visitor John Holden.

PICTURE: JOHN HOLDEN

# ROY SHAW'S WORLD OF AQUATIC FLIES

● The aquatic fly is a vitally important creature to the trout fisherman, who must be able to identify the many different types found on various waters and know the life cycle and behaviour pattern if the right imitation is to be used at the right time on the right day. There are three main orders of flies with roughly the same life cycle. The egg hatches into the nymph, which is a favourite trout food. The nymph goes through several moulting stages before swimming to the surface and emerging as a winged fly know as the dun, which makes for bankside vegetation to shed its outside skin and become a mature adult known as the spinner. When mating has taken place the female deposits her eggs on the water, the adults die and are then known as spent spinners.

PICTURES: ROY SHAW

**ABOVE: Nymph of upwinged fly on ranunculus**

**RIGHT: Large dark olive dun (male)**

**BELOW: Female blue-winged olive with egg ball**

The ageless Fleet Street axiom that one good picture is worth a thousand words was never more true in attempts to show Nature's handiwork in fisheries where hopeful anglers present their lures. Previous editions of Angler's Mail Annual have published masterly studies of Nature at work, as seen through the lens of Roy Shaw's camera. These two pages enhance his reputation with superb close-ups of those aquatic flies which trout anglers strive with skill and patience to copy.

**ABOVE (left): Large dark olive spinners on reed (three males)**

**ABOVE: Brown sedge**

**LEFT: Large dark olive spinner (male)**

ABOVE: Freshwater shrimp (*Gammarus pulex*)

LEFT: Stonefly—willow fly (*Leuctra geniculata*)

No edition of Angler's Mail Annual would be complete without a view of the peaceful natural beauty that surrounds those fortunate enough to enjoy visits to Britain's lovely salmon-fishing rivers. This is Bridge Pool, on the Borrowstone beat of the famous River Dee, Scotland.

PICTURE: ERIC J. CHALKER

Angling continues to attract more women to its ranks and none are more enthusiastic, or successful, than Mrs. Rita Barrett, a Plymouth grandmother, seen here with her catch of an 18 lb. 1 oz. specimen reef pollack, caught from Eddystone Reef. Mrs. Barrett has won many important competitions and is no stranger to Britain's record fish lists.

PICTURE: MIKE MILLMAN

61

FISHING EPISODES

DON'T RELY ON YOUR HUSBANDS SKILL TO PROVIDE A MEAL FOR THE FAMILY

**Don't rely on your husband's skill to provide a meal for the family**

IT'S NO USE YER TRYING WIV BREAD, BILL, THERE'S A BLOKE UP THERE WIV A BIT O' CAKE ON 'IS 'OOK.

# Having a whale of a time!

CLERGYMAN: "My boy, do you know that it's wicked to fish on the Sabbath?"
YOUNGSTER: "I isn't fishin'—I'm teachin' this 'ere wurm ter swim!"

FISHING STRICTLY PROHIBITED

"HERE! CAN'T YOU SEE THAT NOTICE?"
"WELL, I AINT FISHIN'. I'M ONLY TEACHIN' THIS WORM TO SWIM!!"

If your great-grandfather went fishing, it's a fair bet that he chuckled (or winced!) at many of the same jokes about anglers as your grandfather, your father and now you—and possibly your own children. For, as shown in this selection of late Victorian and Edwardian picture postcards, the old jokes live on; only the fashions and surroundings have changed. Mrs. Sylvia Marie Haynes, who loaned these cards for reproduction, is a dedicated collector of old picture postcards, cigarette cards and trade cards for a Museum of Cards which she hopes to establish. Angling humour is just one of the specialised subjects she collects and elsewhere in this edition of Angler's Mail Annual she writes about the history of picture postcards and says that collecting them is now one of the most popular hobbies, with its own dealers, auctions, clubs and magazines.

"Now for a bite"

DONALD :- "LET GO MAN! LET GO! YOU'LL BREAK THE ROD."

A "Bite!"

"A bite at last!"

Is this the disappearing face of sea fishing? Many British lugworm beds are virtually "dug out", so this scene of a typical lugworm dig may well become a nostalgic memory for those whose bait-digging excavations have been part and parcel of their sport.

PICTURE: JOHN HOLDEN

## The Lift Method

*Text by Fred J. Taylor. Illustrations by David Oxford. © IPC Magazines Ltd. 1974. First published in card presentation form by IPC Magazines Ltd. 1974.*

Basically, the lift method is one of the simplest styles of bottom fishing with float tackle. It is unfettered by complicated shotting and, as the name suggests, bites are registered by a lifting of the float in the water, dealing effectively with fast or delicate bites and especially suited to tench fishing. It can be used in slow-moving currents but really excels in stillwaters of moderate depth.

Tackle consists of a length of peacock quill attached to the line at the bottom end only by means of a wide, tight-fitting rubber or plastic band, and cocked by one large shot pinched on the line an inch or so from the baited hook. The tackle is set slightly deeper than the water and the line is tightened to the rod tip after casting, at which stage the float will stand at full cock (fig. 1).

The rod is placed in rod-rests and left there until a bite comes. Any attempt to hold the rod in readiness will cause the float to keel over and the delicate presentation of the bait will be ruined.

When a fish takes the bait from the bottom, the single cocking shot is moved and the anchoring properties are no longer effective. So the natural buoyancy of the quill then takes charge and lifts it up in the water (fig. 2) to fall over flat on the surface (fig. 3).

There are no hard and fast rules regarding the timing of the strike. Sometimes this can be left until the float is lying flat; often, however, the strike must be made while the float is still rising in the water.

The lift method presentation ensures that the bait is always on the bottom, irrespective of the contours of the bed of the lake. Because it is always overloaded, the quill does not support the weight of the shot and this makes it impossible for the float to show on the surface until the bait and shot are anchored to the bottom.

When bites come it is essential to pick up the rod and strike in the one movement. After a little practise this will become second nature.

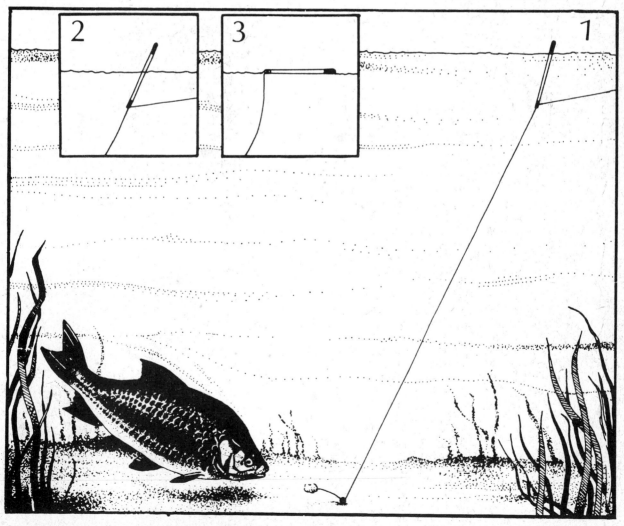

The main drawback with any kind of sliding leger rig that incorporates a one-piece lead is its lack of adjustment to suit prevailing conditions.

Despite other excellent qualities the Arlesey bomb cannot be adjusted to fine limits and there are times when delicate legering requires something

better than the quarter-ounce tolerance between bomb sizes.

The swan-shot link leger was devised for this purpose and progressed through various stages before its present simple and probably more effective form was developed.

The solid leger weight is replaced by a short link of nylon that, preferably, is thicker than the reel line. Simply fold the link into place and secure by a number of swan-shots.

The link will slide freely on the line and can be prevented from slipping down to the hook by any one of a dozen different "stops". The simplest "stop" is a single split shot pinched on above the hook, the distance between hook and link depending upon conditions and bait being used.

Link legers have several advantages over traditional legers, the main one being ease of adjustment. Simply add or remove a swan-shot

## The Link Leger

## The Sliding Float

When water is too deep to fish with a fixed float (and this is generally accepted as being so when the depth is greater than the length of the rod) a sliding float can deal effectively with the situation. But as this is unlikely to be encountered in fast water, the sliding float should generally be regarded as still-water tackle.

Almost any float can be converted into a sliding float, but the most useful is probably the simple antenna-type. The bottom ring attachment allows it to slide freely on the reel line until it comes into contact with a nylon "stop", tied at the desired depth setting.

The advantages are obvious . . . the nylon "stop" passes through the rod rings while casting and with the weight of the terminal tackle concentrated initially at the hook-end, it is easier to place a bait accurately at long-range.

Shotting patterns vary according to the size and carrying capacity of the float but, perhaps, are best split up into three with the main bulk of the shot stationed about 3 ft. from the hook. A single small shot is

pinched on a foot or so above the main shots, so as to hold the float away from them during casting. This shot can be dispensed with entirely on occasions, but in the main it helps prevent tangles in high winds or during long casts.

The final cocking shot, which should take the float down to its proper setting, in pinched on a foot or so below the bulk shot. This delicate shotting pattern will register bites effectively from small fish if the bait is just touching the bottom.

After casting, it may be necessary to put the rod tip under water briefly to ensure that no line remains on the surface to be blown in the wind.

To use the same tackle with the bait hard on the bottom, the shots can be placed nearer the hook and bulked closer together. Bite registration from small fish will be less effective and some from better quality fish may be registered as lift bites, particularly if breadcrust baits are being used.

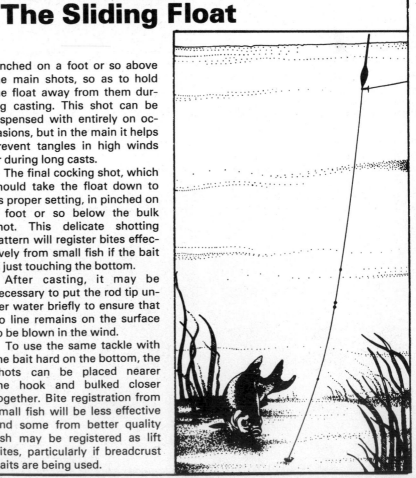

to or from the link so that it "fishes" correctly in the current. Smaller shots can be substituted, if necessary for extremely delicate presentations.

The link leger can be fished up or downstream and is useful in both still and running waters. But as it does not have the streamlined shape of the bomb it is not very good for long range.

One other great advantage of the link leger is that it is virtually snag-proof, particularly in rocky rivers. Most snags occur when the lead, rather than the hook, fouls an obstruction.

Traditional leger tackle often has to be pulled to break but the link leger usually comes free when firm pressure is exerted. The shots slide off the end of the line link and are the only items of tackle lost. The rest comes back intact and fishing can be re-started with little loss of time.

# The Arlesey Bomb Rig

To the best of my knowledge the Arlesey bomb was designed by Richard Walker in the 1950s for long-range perch fishing at Arlesey lake. There were other leger leads in existence at the time but all had the same common failing . . . the line had to pass through the body of the lead and they were prone to tangling during casts. They were not the best of leads for long-range work and seldom lived up to their names as "sliding legers."

The streamlined, swivelled Arlesey bomb lead, perfected after a great deal of experiment, allowed big worm baits to be cast 60 or more yards into deep water, without tangling, and considerably improved bite registration as well. The bomb quickly became the most popular leger lead of all and has been used ever since for every conceivable legering situation.

Choice of weight depends on the distance to be cast or the amount of current to be overcome. Setting on the line depends on the particular fishing situation. For example, the bomb can be stopped a couple of feet from the hook when big lobworms are being used in still-water. Or, it may be necessary to place it no more than two inches from the hook when breadcrust is being used in a fast stream.

To stop the bomb from sliding down to the hook anything from a small split shot to a piece of matchstick or a plastic band can be used. Some anglers prefer to use a separate hook link and to stop the lead by a small split ring. This is a matter for personal choice.

Because of its streamlined shape, the Arlesey bomb is not really suitable for situations where the bait has to be anchored firmly in one spot. But it is ideal for rolling techniques and for near-bank and up-stream legering in rivers. For these situations it is essential to choose a bomb of a weight that will barely counteract the flow of the stream— it should just hold the bottom and no more.

## Dye those maggots— not your fingers!

● Maurice Kausman, the celebrated Huntingdon angler and one of the sport's best-known administrators, wrote in the 1978 edition of Angler's Mail Annual on the subject of baits, colours and odours.

He demonstrated that in his experience fish see colours more definitely in twilight or on a dull day. And in references to the effect of colour on bait he made the simple assumption that a bait which a fish can SEE more clearly is more likely to be taken.

Maurice wrote: "Yellow is the first of the primary colours, as every schoolboy knows. I've proved repeatedly that fish take a yellow maggot more readily than the natural, or any other colour, when the natural light is dull, or fading, as in the evening."

Some anglers report difficulty in dyeing their own maggots, so when talking to match expert Ray Mumford recently, I asked him to explain the methods he uses.

Dye a small quantity of maggots at a time—say a pint at the most. Use good quality maggots and riddle them through a sieve to remove sawdust and bran.

When the maggots are free from dust lay them in a shallow bait container—the plastic Efgeeco type is probably the best. Sprinkle the maggots with two teaspoonfuls of water and then stir them to dampen their skins.

Measure out one-quarter of a teaspoon of Chrysodine dye, which is obtainable from tackle shops for about 50p a tube, and lightly sprinkle it over the maggots.

Stir up the maggots with the teaspoon (NOT your fingers!) to make sure they are all covered in dye and then put the lid on the bait container.

Leave for 15 minutes and then check that the maggots are colouring up. Leave for a further 45 minutes to make sure all the maggots are properly dyed and then transfer them to a dry container. Add one or two handfuls of bran to dry the maggots right out.

Maggots should never be retained in a wet container because, if left for a period of time, they can clean themselves.

*Note:* Auramine O for pale yellow; Rhodamine B for red and Bismarck Brown for brown maggots.

**MELVYN RUSS**

# Spot the difference

*Written and illustrated by David Carl Forbes* © IPC Magazines Ltd. 1974

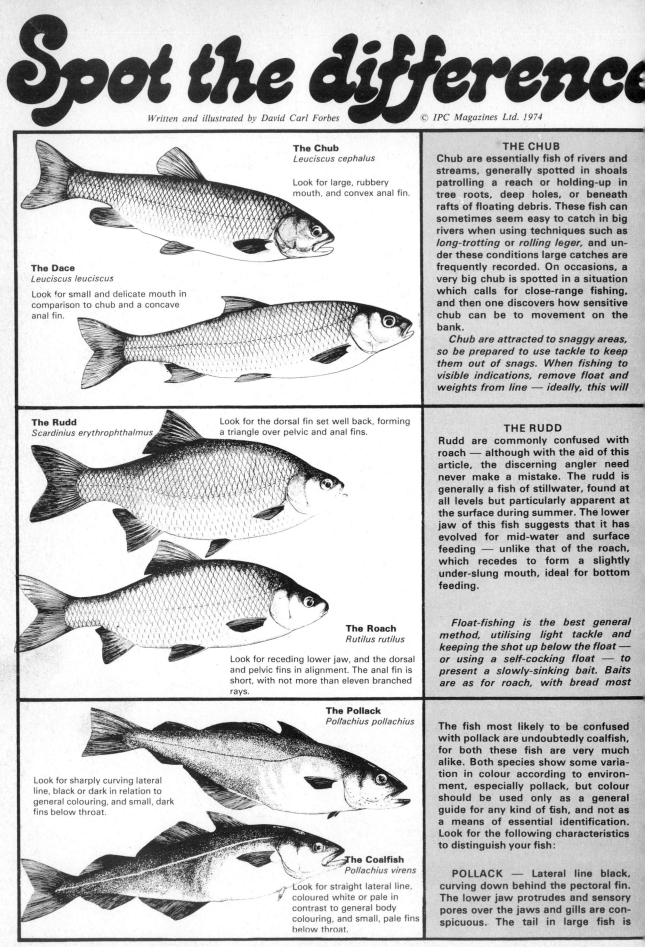

**The Chub**
*Leuciscus cephalus*

Look for large, rubbery mouth, and convex anal fin.

**The Dace**
*Leuciscus leuciscus*

Look for small and delicate mouth in comparison to chub and a concave anal fin.

**The Rudd**
*Scardinius erythrophthalmus*

Look for the dorsal fin set well back, forming a triangle over pelvic and anal fins.

**The Roach**
*Rutilus rutilus*

Look for receding lower jaw, and the dorsal and pelvic fins in alignment. The anal fin is short, with not more than eleven branched rays.

**The Pollack**
*Pollachius pollachius*

Look for sharply curving lateral line, black or dark in relation to general colouring, and small, dark fins below throat.

**The Coalfish**
*Pollachius virens*

Look for straight lateral line, coloured white or pale in contrast to general body colouring, and small, pale fins below throat.

## THE CHUB

Chub are essentially fish of rivers and streams, generally spotted in shoals patrolling a reach or holding-up in tree roots, deep holes, or beneath rafts of floating debris. These fish can sometimes seem easy to catch in big rivers when using techniques such as *long-trotting* or *rolling leger,* and under these conditions large catches are frequently recorded. On occasions, a very big chub is spotted in a situation which calls for close-range fishing, and then one discovers how sensitive chub can be to movement on the bank.

*Chub are attracted to snaggy areas, so be prepared to use tackle to keep them out of snags. When fishing to visible indications, remove float and weights from line — ideally, this will*

## THE RUDD

Rudd are commonly confused with roach — although with the aid of this article, the discerning angler need never make a mistake. The rudd is generally a fish of stillwater, found at all levels but particularly apparent at the surface during summer. The lower jaw of this fish suggests that it has evolved for mid-water and surface feeding — unlike that of the roach, which recedes to form a slightly under-slung mouth, ideal for bottom feeding.

*Float-fishing is the best general method, utilising light tackle and keeping the shot up below the float — or using a self-cocking float — to present a slowly-sinking bait. Baits are as for roach, with bread most*

The fish most likely to be confused with pollack are undoubtedly coalfish, for both these fish are very much alike. Both species show some variation in colour according to environment, especially pollack, but colour should be used only as a general guide for any kind of fish, and not as a means of essential identification. Look for the following characteristics to distinguish your fish:

**POLLACK** — Lateral line black, curving down behind the pectoral fin. The lower jaw protrudes and sensory pores over the jaws and gills are conspicuous. The tail in large fish is

Newcomers (and some old hands) in coarse fishing often mistake a small chub for a big dace, or get muddled between a roach and a rudd. Sea anglers, too, are sometimes in a tangle when it comes to quick and accurate identification of look-alike species, such as pollack and coalfish.

The late David Carl Forbes, a gifted artist and skilful angler, prepared the text and drawings featured here for presentation cards promoted by Angler's Mail in 1974. They are reprinted in this edition of the Annual to preserve the work in more permanent form and to help young anglers and newcomers.

be 4 or 5 lb. b.s. — and rely upon the weight of the bait for casting. Baits can be whole lobworms, slugs, garden snails, cubes of luncheon meat, large balls of bread or cheese for this form of fishing. Hooks should be in keeping with the size of the bait, ranging from size 10 to size 4 — strike hard to set these larger hooks. In open water situations, baits such as maggots, or bread flake, may be float-fished on light tackle.

Approach chub swims with extreme caution, even crawling into position if necessary, and keep all movements to a minimum. Do step-up tackle throughout for chub in snaggy waters, and consider that a medium-sized chub may be much larger than any fish you are normally likely to catch on your general coarse-

fishing tackle. Really big chub may be encountered even in very small waters.

## THE DACE

Shoal fish of moving water, dace are generally encountered in fast, shallow runs over gravel, although outstandingly large fish may be caught in deep holes and slacks. In most waters, the really big fish move in shoals of ten or twelve, while average fish may be in shoals of two or three hundred. In chalk-streams like the Hampshire Avon, dace of all sizes may be seen in many hundreds in the shallows, particularly near the end of the season as spawning time approaches.

*Try long-trotting with light tackle, ground-baiting little and often, to get big catches. For this form of fishing, employ a suitable float to trot well in*

*fast water and use hooks between size 18 and size 12, baited with single or double maggot. Maggots are top bait for sheer numbers of fish on most waters, with bread producing individually larger fish.*

Do make a point of gauging the groundbait according to the flow of the current. Too much at a time may take the shoal chasing off after particles downstream. Too little, and the shoal may work upstream in search of more, until they are under your rod-tip and thus easily frightened.

Look for that distinctive anal fin when confronted with what appears to be a huge dace — you might be able to claim a local record, or save yourself the embarrassment of reporting what is merely a very small chub.

generally effective. Rudd have much larger mouths than roach, mouths better adapted to take a relatively large bait easily and quickly. For fish in excess of 8 oz., tear an inch square of bread from a sliced loaf to fold over a size 10 or size 8 hook as flake. No need for tiny hooks in baits of this size! On occasions, at the peak of summer, fly fishing can account for good rudd.

Make a cautious approach to the water, keep down off the sky-line, and cast smoothly to reduce the risk of the hook tangling up around the float. For big catches, use cloud or light groundbait to keep fish working mid-water, rather than floating bread, that keeps fish on surface where they will eventually be frightened by your movements.

## THE ROACH

This is the common fish of British freshwater. Easily caught when small, with age and increased size it becomes the most difficult of quarry. Roach are found in all waters, from tiny ponds to great rivers — and the size of the water does not necessarily determine the size of the fish.

Inevitably, anglers of all ages and ability catch roach, but few anglers consistently catch big roach. These fish are shy creatures, often unseen even by experienced anglers and are the reward of patient and discerning angling.

*Move into a swim with extreme caution and use tackle as streamlined and as light as conditions will allow. Float-fishing is invariably best, using a long rod with, as a general guide, 3 lb. b.s. line, a sensitive float, and*

hooks ranging from size 18 up to size 10, depending upon bait. Bread, maggots, or lobworm tails are generally effective baits, according to the nature of the water. With maggots, use a single bait on a size 18 or 16 hook. With bread, or worm, employ the larger hooks.

Fish close to, or right on the bottom, using *long-trotting* technique in moving water and *laying-on* in stillwater. Roach may be caught throughout the year, even in severe winters and, in fact, these offer the best chance of big fish. Search out the channels between weed in rivers in summer, and explore gullies and deep holes in pits and lakes during winter. Roach come from all types of swims, but avoid beds of loose mud or concentrations of decaying leaves.

squared, and the tiny fins below the throat are dark, without filaments.

**COALFISH** — Lateral line white and virtually straight from gills to root of tail. The lower jaw protrudes in very large fish, but not to the same extent as pollack. The tail is forked and the fins below the throat are white, extending into small filaments. There is a minute 'beard' — absent in the pollack — but this is so small that it will be seen only by careful inspection.

Pollack and coalfish may be found together in the same areas, although the pollack is more widely and

generously distributed — with the cream of the fishing coming from Irish and West Country waters. The greatest concentrations of coalfish appear to occur in northern waters. Pollack are particularly associated with rocky ledges. out-crops and wrecks, tending to hold-up near these obstructions and ambush rather than rove in search of food, and the big specimens consistently fall to boat anglers.

*The best baits are moving baits — small fish, fish strips, all manner of lures such as rubber sand-eels, feathers, and so on — and these*

*should be worked in erratic, jerking movement. The fairly general idea of leaving tackle to 'fish for itself' will not often produce pollack or coalfish, and the ideal is to keep the bait fluttering and jerking — thinking in terms of the movement, rather than the actual bait, attracting the fish.*

Fishing for shad under the salmon ladder at Tewkesbury Weir, on the River Severn.

# THE SHAD MYSTERY

## By RON FELTON

THE mysterious shad will make its annual dash up the Severn early in May and reports of the first rod and line catches will quickly follow. But just why the shad — a sort of overgrown herring — should make this annual Spring pilgrimage, along with the salmon and elvers, is open to speculation.

Many anglers believe the shad are simply following the elvers and feeding upon them. But in some seasons the shad do not appear until several weeks after the elver run has finished.

I think the real reason why these fish enter a freshwater environment must be connected with spawning. I have observed vast shoals of shad making rapid, circular movements on the surface of the water and I am convinced this behaviour is associated with the spawning cycle.

But the mystery remains since I have never seen or heard of any shad fry in the river. And it is also uncertain whether the adult fish perish in the Severn or return to the sea.

What is clear is that there are two species of shad — the twaite and the allis. The twaite can be recognised by distinctive markings, almost like portholes down its flank.

In low river conditions the shad become trapped below the Severn weirs, or in shallow rapids on such rivers as the Wye and Usk.

The most popular Severnside centre is Tewkesbury Weir and that's where I was joined by fellow Birmingham anglers Graeme Edge and John Williams for a boat-fishing session. And although the river was two feet above normal we still managed to catch a good bag of shad, using home-made fly spoons.

The Tewkesbury shad shoals were waiting for high spring tides, or a further rise in river height through rain, which would allow them to negotiate the weir and continue their journey upstream.

Home-made fly spoons, fashioned from aluminium and brass sheet, are successful shad lures.

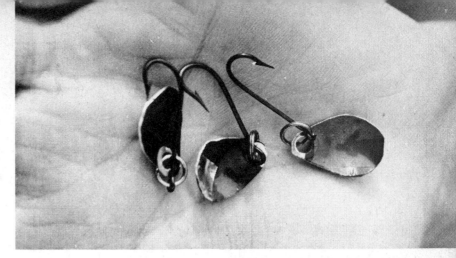

How about that then? Young Stephen Felton proudly displays a shad.

Gotcha! A Severn shad is safely netted.

Shad are great favourites with the local angling club, Tewkesbury Popler, who control the fishing on the Tewkesbury side and reserve the weir for members only. A limited number of day-tickets are available which permit visitors to fish some distance from the weir. The favourite method of shad fishing is to use a fly spoon with about 6 lb. line. Three or four shots are pinched on the trace and the spoon retrieved as close to the bottom as possible.

Shad will also take wet fly or a small piece of silver paper attached to an ordinary hook. The bites are unmistakable although the shad's mouth is tough and they easily shed the hook.

# NATIONAL ANGLING

THE annual series of Divisional Championships organised by the National Federation of Anglers was extended to four Divisions in 1978, involving 265 teams from affiliated clubs.

The championships were born on the banks of the River Thames in 1906, when seven teams assembled at Pangbourne and weighed-in a total of 17 lb. 8¼ oz.

By 1971 the single annual event had grown to 116 teams and the NFA re-organised the contest into two Divisions, which operated from 1972 to 1974. A third Division was added in 1975.

Promotion and relegation operates within the Divisions on the basis of 10 up and 10 down, with the results of the teams competition currently decided on a points basis.

Top weight in each section gains the same number of points as there are teams competing, the second highest receives one point less and so on, with nil points if a team fails to catch any fish or for absent or disqualified members.

The Angler's Mail Annual Championships Table shows the winning teams and top individual competitors from the start in 1906 to 1978—the latest results to hand when this edition went to press.

**Top man in the National Federation's Division I Championship was Dave Harris, of Bradford, with a bream catch of 48 lb. 13 oz., from the Bristol Avon.**

**The 1978 Division II champion was Ivan Carrier, of Long Eaton, Notts., who won with 10 lb. 15½ oz. and is pictured with two of his trophies.**

**Rushden angler Peter Laughton gives a fond farewell to one of the nine bream that helped him to weigh-in 26 lb. 12½ oz., and gain second place in the NFA Division III Championship on the River Witham in August, 1978.**

**A Fourth Division was added in 1978 to the annual team and individual championships organised by the National Federation of Anglers. The first winners were Swindon Talisman team, seen here with their awards. They weighed-in 30 lb. 1 oz., from the West Country's River Huntspill and the South and King's Sedgemoor Drains, Somerset.**

## N.F.A. DIVISIONAL CHAMPIONSHIPS

| Date | Venue | Teams | Winners | Team weight | | | Individual highest weight | | |
|------|-------|-------|---------|------|------|------|---------------------------|------|------|
| | | | | lb | oz | dr | | lb | oz | dr |
| 1906 | R. Thames, Pangbourne | 7 | Boston | 17 | 8 | 4 | F. Beales (Boston) | 4 | 11 | 0 |
| 1907 | R. Witham, Kirkstead | 13 | Sheffield Amal. | 21 | 12 | 12 | A. Croft (Sheffield) | 7 | 1 | 8 |
| 1908 | North Level Drain, Tydd | 13 | Sheffield & Dist. | 18 | 6 | 0 | J. Mason (Sheffield) | 12 | 2 | 0 |
| 1909 | The Dyke, Newark, Notts. | 18 | Leeds Amal. | 7 | 5 | 4 | J. H. R. Bazley (Leeds) | 2 | 2 | 8 |
| 1910 | R. Derwent, Hutton's Ambo | 17 | Leeds Amal. | 5 | 8 | 12 | A. Blackman (Hull) | 2 | 13 | 8 |
| 1911 | R. Severn, Kimpsey | 19 | Sheffield Amal. | 53 | 6 | 0 | W. Lowe (Sheffield) | 13 | 4 | 0 |
| 1912 | R. Ouse, Ely | 20 | Boston | 25 | 9 | 0 | G. Beales (Boston) | 6 | 11 | 12 |
| 1913 | R. Dee, Chester | 22 | Nottingham | 2 | 15 | 0 | W. Gough (Nottingham) | 1 | 14 | 8 |
| 1914 | R. Trent, Willington | 20 | Leeds Amal. | 20 | 14 | 8 | A. Skerratt (Derby) | 6 | 15 | 12 |
| 1919 | R. Ancholme, Brigg | 24 | Boston | 20 | 0 | 8 | T. Hill (Derby) | 7 | 7 | 0 |
| 1920 | R. Weaver, Hartford | 29 | County Palatine | 12 | 4 | 0 | R. Barlow (Hull) | 3 | 1 | 0 |
| 1921 | R. Trent, Burton Joyce | 32 | Derby | 10 | 1 | 0 | J. Wakesfield (Derby) | 6 | 2 | 12 |
| 1922 | R. Witham, Kirkstead | 38 | Lincoln | 10 | 5 | 12 | B. Hobday (Lincoln) | 3 | 5 | 8 |
| 1923 | R. Soar, Kegworth | 41 | County Palatine | 18 | 11 | 0 | J. W. Couldwell (Sheffield) | 5 | 15 | 8 |
| 1924 | R. Glen, Pinchbeck, Lincs. | 43 | Castleford & Dist. | 28 | 0 | 8 | W. T. Willcocks (London) | 21 | 8 | 8 |
| 1925 | R. Severn, Worcester | 46 | Long Eaton | 5 | 10 | 8 | G. Allen (Provincial) | 3 | 8 | 12 |
| 1926 | R. Ouse, Naburn, Yorks. | 47 | Lincoln | 23 | 11 | 9 | A. Fletcher (Boston) | 7 | 1 | 0 |
| 1927 | Middle Level Drain, King's Lynn, Norfolk | 47 | Grimsby & Dist. | 44 | 5 | 12 | J. H. R. Bazley (Leeds) | 16 | 5 | 8 |
| 1928 | R. Severn, Tewkesbury, Glos. | 44 | Leeds & Dist. | 13 | 2 | 13 | W. Tetley (Leeds) | 3 | 13 | 3 |
| 1929 | R. Witham, Kirkstead, Lincs. | 44 | Boston | 50 | 4 | 0 | J. Sykes (Boston) | 10 | 15 | 0 |
| 1930 | R. Soar, Kegworth, Derby | 51 | Sheffield Amal. | 43 | 10 | 0 | C. Muddimer (Leicester) | 15 | 6 | 0 |
| 1931 | South Forty Foot Drain | 48 | Hull Amal. | 27 | 9 | 8 | O. Daddy (Hull) | 18 | 9 | 8 |
| 1932 | R. Soar, Kegworth, Derby | 47 | Loughborough | 24 | 15 | 0 | H. Sallis (Long Eaton) | 5 | 9 | 4 |
| 1933 | R. Great Ouse, Olney, Bucks. | 48 | Sheffield & Dist. | 33 | 6 | 4 | Edgar Dabill (Sheffield) | 13 | 15 | 9 |
| 1934 | R. Thames, Abingdon, Berks. | 54 | Sheffield Amal. | 14 | 3 | 11 | H. Smith (Sheffield) | 4 | 14 | 4 |
| 1935 | R. Witham, Kirkstead, Lincs. | 50 | Lincoln | 43 | 13 | 2 | A. Kellett (Doncaster) | 18 | 6 | 15 |
| 1936 | R. Thurne, Potter Heigham | 53 | Lincoln | 74 | 5 | 15 | A. E. Bryant (Buckingham) | 35 | 1 | 0 |
| 1937 | Gloucester Canal | 56 | Groves & Whitnall | 23 | 15 | 6 | H. Jones (Co. Palatine) | 9 | 9 | 9 |
| 1938 | R. Great Ouse, Harrold | 62 | Hull & Dist. | 38 | 12 | 7 | G. Bright (Bistol) | 21 | 13 | 8 |
| 1945 | R. Trent, Newark, Notts. | 57 | Worksop | 75 | 2 | 5 | M. T. Cotteril (Worksop) | 16 | 1 | 7 |
| 1946 | R. Witham, Langrick, Notts. | 66 | Hull | 57 | 0 | 12 | G. Laybourne (York) | 12 | 12 | 8 |
| 1947 | R. Witham, Kirkstead, Lincs. | 70 | Worksop | 57 | 8 | 4 | W. Edwards (Rotherham) | 9 | 4 | 8 |
| 1948 | R. Huntspill, Somerset | 72 | Leeds Amal. | 23 | 14 | 4 | W. Thompson (Leeds) | 14 | 9 | 12 |
| 1949 | R. Thurne, Potter Heigham | 77 | Leeds Amal. | 49 | 3 | 4 | R. Woodhall (Whit. Reans) | 15 | 6 | 8 |
| 1950 | R. Nene, Peterborough | 81 | Peterborough | 62 | 5 | 12 | W. Rockley (Peterborough) | 15 | 4 | 0 |
| 1951 | R. Witham, Kirkstead, Lincs. | 82 | Doncaster | 93 | 5 | 0 | S. Buxton (Doncaster) | 20 | 13 | 4 |
| 1952 | R. Severn, Bridgnorth, Salop | 88 | Leeds Amal. | 135 | 5 | 0 | H. Seed (Leeds) | 33 | 5 | 4 |
| 1953 | R. Nene, Peterborough | 92 | Lincoln | 72 | 5 | 0 | N. N. Hazelwood (Cmb.) | 27 | 14 | 0 |
| 1954 | R. Trent, Gunthorpe, Notts. | 98 | Hull Angling Pres. | 68 | 13 | 1 | R. Lye (Notts. Fed.) | 15 | 1 | 12 |
| 1955 | R. Huntspill, Bridgwater, Som. | 99 | Sheffield Amal. | 136 | 15 | 4 | J. Carr (Sheffield Amal.) | 68 | 2 | 4 |
| 1956 | R. Witham, Kirkstead, Lincs. | 94 | Coventry & Dist. | 86 | 4 | 4 | C. R. Lusby (Lincoln) | 25 | 8 | 0 |
| 1957 | R. Severn, Bridgnorth, Salop. | 96 | Notts. A.A. | 22 | 8 | 1 | H. Storey (Notts. A.A.) | 7 | 12 | 8 |
| 1958 | R. Welland, Spalding, Lincs. | 98 | Coventry A.A. | 59 | 15 | 4 | W. Hughes (Northern Anglers) | 24 | 3 | 0 |
| 1959 | R. Nene, Peterborough | 100 | Bedford A.C. | 86 | 1 | 4 | J. Sharp (Bedford) | 57 | 8 | 3 |
| 1960 | Rs. Ant, Bure, Thurne, Nflk. | 101 | King's Lynn A.A. | 81 | 15 | 1 | K. Smith (Norwich) | 50 | 14 | 8 |
| 1961 | R. Trent, Nottingham | 103 | Coventry A.A. | 77 | 6 | 12 | J. Blakey (Saltaire) | 23 | 12 | 12 |
| 1962 | R. Welland, Spalding, Lincs. | 103 | Lincoln | 56 | 2 | 12 | V. A. Baker (Derby Railway) | 13 | 11 | 0 |
| 1963 | Gloucester Canal | 105 | Northampton Nene A.C. | 19 | 11 | 2 | R. Sims (N. Som. & West Wilts.) | 14 | 15 | 2 |
| 1964 | R. Severn, Worcester | 107 | Kidderminster | 50 | 13 | 2 | G. Burch (Essex County) | 32 | 3 | 0 |
| 1965 | R. Huntspill, Somerset | 110 | Rugby Federation | 93 | 7 | 8 | D. Burr (Rugby) | 76 | 9 | 0 |
| 1966 | R. Witham, Lincs. | 108 | Boston | 75 | 1 | 4 | R. Jarvis (Boston) | 29 | 1 | 8 |
| 1967 | Relief Channel, Norfolk | 111 | Derby Railway | 83 | 4 | 4 | E. Townsin (Cambridge F.P.) | 40 | 6 | 8 |
| 1968 | Rs. Ant, Bure, Thurne, Nflk. | 112 | Leighton Buzzard | 74 | 0 | 8 | D. Groom (Leighton Buzzard) | 36 | 6 | 0 |
| 1969 | R. Trent, Nottingham | 114 | Stoke | 32 | 8 | 2 | R. Else (Lincoln) | 9 | 7 | 3 |
| 1970 | Middle Level Drain | 113 | Cambridge FPS | 97 | 2 | 0 | B. Lakey (Cambridge) | 35 | 4 | 8 |
| 1971 | R. Severn, Stourport | 116 | Leicester | 124 | 8 | 8 | R. Harris (Peterborough) | 40 | 5 | 0 |

| Date | Venue | Teams | Winners | Team weight | | | Team points | Individual highest weight | lb | oz | dr |
|---|---|---|---|---|---|---|---|---|---|---|---|
| | | | | lb | oz | dr | | | | | |
| 1972 | Div. 1: Bristol Avon | 79 | Birmingham A.A. | 51 | 1 | 12 | 248 | P. Coles (Leicester) | 33 | 8 | 0 |
| | Div. 2: R. Welland | 81 | Coleshill, Warwks. | 72 | 15 | 8 | 216 | J. Hart (Whittlesey, Cambs.) | 54 | 14 | 8 |
| 1973 | Div. 1: R. Witham | 80 | Grimsby A.S.A. | 92 | 10 | 4 | 717 | A. Wright (Derby Rly. Inst.) | 41 | 10 | 8 |
| | Div. 2: Gt. Ouse Relief Channel | 92 | Leigh & Dist. (Lancs.) | 76 | 6 | 8 | 826 | J. Wilkinson (Elthorne A.S., Hanwell) | 43 | 1 | 8 |
| 1974 | Div. 1: R. Welland | 80 | Leicester A.S. | 25 | 9 | 4 | 733 | P. Anderson (Cambridge F.P.A.S.) | 40 | 2 | 8 |
| | Div. 2: R. Avon (Warwks.) | 85 | Stockport Fed. | 71 | 0 | 8 | 1161 | C. Hibbs (Leigh Miners) | 47 | 3 | 8 |
| 1975 | Div. 1: R. Nene | 79 | Birmingham A.A. | 43 | 15 | 12 | 814 | M. Hoad-Reddick (Rotherham U.A.F.) | 63 | 7 | 0 |
| | Div. 2: R. Trent | 71 | Long Eaton Victoria A.S., Nottingham | 60 | 6 | 4 | 735 | A. Webber (Wigan) | 16 | 2 | 8 |
| | Div. 3: R. Welland | 42 | Crawley A.S., Sussex | 18 | 9 | 0 | 394 | J. Garrett (GEC Marconi, Chelmsford) | 24 | 8 | 0 |
| 1976 | Div. 1: R. Trent | 79 | Birmingham A.A. | 53 | 14 | 4 | 776 | N. Wells (Newark) | 28 | 0 | 8 |
| | Div. 2: R. Witham | 76 | Izaak Walton (Preston) A.S. | 34 | 14 | 8 | 783 | P. Marks (Exeter) | 12 | 11 | 8 |
| | Div. 3: R. Huntspill, South and King's Sedgemoor Drains | 80 | London A.A. | 47 | 6 | 4 | 693 | D. Knox (Cheadle) | 38 | 9 | 12 |
| 1977 | Div. 1: R. Welland | 77 | Coventry A.A. | 24 | 15 | 4 | 755 | R. Foster (Rotherham) | 39 | 10 | 4 |
| | Div. 2: Grt. Ouse | 72 | Huntingdon A.S. | 34 | 10 | 12 | 687 | S. Yoemans (Reading) | 24 | 3 | 0 |
| | Div. 3: R. Trent | 90 | Stratford upon Avon A.A. | 30 | 9 | 0 | 881 | C. Robinson (Barnet) | 18 | 4 | 8 |
| 1978 | Div. 1: Bristol Avon | 79 | Coleshill & Dist. A.S. | 84 | 11 | 8 | 790 | D. Harris (Bradford City) | 48 | 13 | 0 |
| | Div. 2: R. Trent | 78 | Nottingham A.A. | 36 | 13 | 4 | 806 | I. Carrier (Long Eaton) | 10 | 5 | 8 |
| | Div. 3: R. Witham | 74 | Bathampton A.A. | 33 | 13 | 4 | 712 | L. Constable (Chatteris) | 29 | 8 | 8 |
| | Div. 4: R. Huntspill, South and King's Sedgemoor Drains | 34 | Swindon Talisman A.C. | 30 | 1 | 0 | 353 | B. Shepherd (Ramsey & Dist A.C.) | 56 | 2 | 0 |

# N.F.A LADIES NATIONAL CHAMPIONSHIPS

AVIS THOMAS from Leeds—wife of the 1977/8 Angler's Mail Matchman of the Year star Dave Thomas—made it a family double when she won the NFA Ladies National on the upper River Nene with a 2 lb. 7 oz. catch of tiny roach, "skimmer" bream, gudgeon and perch.

She was the only woman to weigh-in more than 2 lb. of fish along the whole Elton and Nassington length of the Nene.

Runner-up was Sheffield shop assistant Pat Needham, who took 1-12-0 to the scales. Third place went to Chesterfield tackle dealer Gladys Evans, 36, who snatched 1-9-0 of bleak on a 22-foot long pole.

**Smiling Avis Thomas, the 1978 Ladies Angling Champion, holds her glittering prizes.**

# NATIONAL JUNIOR CHAMPIONSHIP

A team of youngsters from Stockport, Cheshire, raced to a brilliant win in the 1978 National Junior Championships, held on the Leeds-Liverpool canal. They scored 611 points to beat their arch rivals from Birmingham, who finished second.

Individual winner Alan Hunt, 15, of Coventry, fished in masterful style on the gin-clear canal at Aintree to catch seven tench and a few roach totalling 8 lb. 4 oz.

Tench also figured in the second-placed individual catch of 5 lb. 9 oz., made by Wakefield's Mark Wade, 15. Birmingham skipper Felix Evans, 15, was third individual with 5 lb. 6 oz.

Victory smiles all round as the National Junior Champions from Stockport and District pose with their prizes after winning the 1978 title on the Leeds-Liverpool Canal.

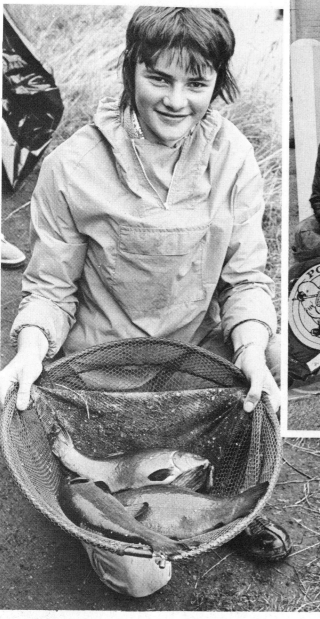

Alan Hunt, 15, from Coventry, won the 1978 Junior "National" with this catch of 8 lb. 4 oz., from the Leeds-Liverpool canal.

| Date | Venue | Teams | Winners | Team weight | | | Team points | Individual highest weight | | | |
|------|-------|-------|---------|----|----|----|------|---------------------------|----|----|----|
| | | | | lb | oz | dr | | | lb | oz | dr |
| 1978 | Leeds-Liverpool canal | 56 | Stockport and Dist. | 21 | 1 | 4 | 611 | A. Hunt (Coventry) | 8 | 4 | 0 |

Bathampton captain Mike Jones took this 6 lb. $14\frac{1}{2}$ oz. catch to win top individual place in the East Anglian Cup final on the River Trent.

# EAST ANGLIAN KNOCKOUT CUP

Bathampton AA made it a great season for the South-West clubs when the won the East Anglian Knockout Tournament.

Against all the odds, Bathampton defeated favourites from Lincoln in the final, held on Walter Bower's North Muskham stretch of the River Trent, near Newark, to win the £5,000 event, sponsored by the East Anglian Rod Company.

Early heats were held at local level within the eight NFA Regions and once a small nucleus of surviving teams was left from an original entry of more than 100 teams, the ties were fished on a national basis—involving some squads in major expeditions across the length and breadth of the country, to fish at venues new to them.

The Bathampton team celebrate their shock East Anglian Cup victory with a champagne "shower"—courtesy of team stalwart Mervyn Haskins.

# MATCHMAN OF THE YEAR

THE first Matchman of the Year contest was devised and presented by Angler's Mail for the 1977–78 coarse fishing season up to March 14, 1978.

It was an immediate success and acclaimed as the first nationally-organised attempt to seek out the most consistently successful match-fishing performers over a full season—in direct contrast to major national competitions which tend to offer instant fame and substantial rewards for a solo performance in a single event.

Vigilant monitoring of published results of every bona fide Open match, with at least 100 anglers taking part, built up a fascinating dossier of determination and talent as the weeks went by.

Ten points were awarded for every win in an eligible Open event, five points for second place and two for a third.

Some of the biggest names in the sport slipped down the points ladder as the huge initial climb produced a smaller pack of front runners.

Winner Dave Thomas, of Leeds, scored 63 points with four Firsts, three Seconds and four Thirds. It was a popular victory and lead to immediate recognition of consistency when Dave was invited to join the England squad for the World Championships in Vienna in the autumn of 1978.

Runner-up Billy Makin, from Atherstone, Warwicks., scored 60 points, with Colin Perry, of Mansfield, and John Illingworth, of Bradford, in joint third place with 35 points each.

Matchman of the Year in the 1978–1979 season, up to March 14, 1979, had several weeks still to run when this edition of the Annual went to press. But the competition was enhanced by a £3,000 sponsorship by the Shakespeare tackle company, making the event one of the most valuable match purses in the United Kingdom.

**Congratulations from one champion to another as Leeds ace Dave Thomas holds the magnificent Kent Trophy that went with the title of Angler's Mail Matchman of the Year in 1977–78 season . . . and gets a kiss from his wife Avis, who won the 1978 Ladies Championship on the River Nene.**

# WHERE DO YOU LOOK FOR BIG BREAM?

*Peter Stone's pointers to the right places*

**B**IG bream capture the imagination of so many anglers but the initial problem for most is to find a water that holds fish of the right size.

Do you go to a small lake where location is easier, or to a bigger pit which may hold larger fish?

But what qualifies as a big bream, anyway? In my book, anything over 6 lb., but for the purpose of this exercise let's aim a little higher — say 8 lb. The reason for this is the effect that catching a bream has on its growth rate, for I'm certain that when a 6 lb. bream is caught, unhooked and returned, its growth rate is retarded to the extent that it may never reach double-figures.

Big waters or small? Two factors must be considered. Big waters of 30 acres or larger are much more likely to produce double-figure fish than small ones. But on big pits much of the water remains virgin territory unless you have access to a boat.

Big waters produce heavyweight bream fairly regularly but bear in mind that actual numbers taken may be quite small.

If a water has depths of 12 ft. or more so much the better, as I find that big bream love deep water, though they may not be there all the time.

A big fish by any standards. Peter with a 9 lb. stillwater bream.

Another feature to look for is gin-clear water, which is why I now fish gravel pits such a lot. Weedy or clear water? — I'm not fussy. I have taken big bream from both.

Bank contours are important in big waters. In my experience, big bream tend to stay well out from the bank — 25 yards or more — and for much of the time they are well beyond effective fishing range. So I don't go for corners or bays. Peninsulas and points are what I look for, places which permit me to cast well out — and, hopefully, intercept the passing shoals.

On small waters the all-important factor is fishing pressure. If it is heavy I don't fancy them, although if big bream are occasionally caught the water is obviously worth investigating. Even so, unless I could fish at night with few other anglers doing likewise, I would look for something better. Small, heavily-fished waters do not produce big bream very often.

Small, virgin pits I like. These are the waters that often turn up big bream for those who fish them first — skimming the cream as it were. Small pits need not be deep nor weedy; if the water is pure the bream wax fat and big.

A typical example of this occurred at a small pit I know. The pit is rarely fished by serious anglers, but a trial netting in a summer drought turned up a 9 lb. bream. I knew the water, but it had never excited me as a place for big bream.

**The rewards of finding the right water. This trio weighed 10 lb., 9½ lb. and 9 lb. 2 oz.**

If you can find such a small water, get permission to fish it, or, if acquired by a club, be among the first to fish there and you could be in business. Should it become heavily fished later on it might prove a one-off affair. In my experience, once a few big bream get caught they quickly become wary.

Now to the last — and what I consider one of the most important factors.

Lakes, meres or pits, which are capable of the occasional bream over say, 7 lb., but caught only by matchmen or pleasure anglers, are definitely waters which can produce some very big bream, if approached in the right manner.

If such a water is big and contains unfished areas—so much the better. But it does not have to be big; small waters can be just as profitable.

Several years ago a pleasure angler told me of a water from which he had taken a few bream of 7 lb., I concentrated on that water immediately, put everything together and began to catch bream between 8 lb. and 10 lb. But the word got around and they became much harder to find.

The late Bill Keal once said that a double-figure bream was the hardest fish of all to catch. I think he was right, for the problems are indeed complex. Some of these I have solved; others I haven't. But, as always, choosing the right water is the first essential.

Some of the more interesting books from the collection. Bottom left is a first edition of William Bailey's "Angler Instructor" published in 1857, the bookplate showed that it once belonged to O. M. Reed a well-known angling writer of some 40 years ago. Next to it is a handsome first edition of Bickerdyke's classic. In the top row is one of the very first books on roach fishing, a signed first edition of J. W. Martin, who wrote under the pen name of Trent Otter, and an early copy of H. Cholmondeley-Pennell's "Fishing Gossip".

My collecting has always had a fishy flavour—old rods, reels and other bits and pieces. But my chief interest is in old books . . . clean copies of those dog-eared volumes I borrowed from the library as a lad and whose advice and instruction set me on the path to becoming a dedicated angler.

Collecting angling books is a hobby which can grip as tightly as the sport itself. It gives a great deal of pleasure, a touch of nostalgia and it's a good form of investment. Old books can only become scarcer so the pre-war book that now costs £1 will be worth double in a year or so. That's good value when you consider that most modern paperbacks sell for £1 and usually end up in the dustbin. What's more, a library of good fishing books makes an attractive addition to the living room where, on those cold, dark winter evenings, you can relax with a handsome volume and read what yesterday's anglers had to say about fishing.

The secondhand stall at your local market may well turn up an old fishing book priced at 20p but really worth 50 times that sum. After the first couple of volumes it's amazing how quickly a collection can grow. My own started with a tattered copy of L. A. Parker's "This Fishing", bought about ten years ago. Now I have more than 300 books.

Don't be put off because everything old now seems to cost a lot of money. Very early books can be expensive and so can limited, signed first editions of some of the classics. But if you know where to look you can still buy a good book for the price of a packet of cigarettes.

If money is limited, the best place to start is a local jumble sale, junk shop or street market. You may have to sort through hundreds of volumes of pulp fiction and children's Annuals before finding what you want but it will turn up eventually. Don't take too much notice of the wiseacres who say that dealers pick up all the bargains in such places. General dealers scour the markets and junk shops for gold, silver jewellery, oil lamps and bric-a-brac for ready sale. But they rarely have the time or knowledge to sort through for book bargains and that gives the amateur collector plenty of opportunities.

Disappointments are part of the collecting game. You could pay a weekly visit to the same junk stall for months on end without finding anything and then, just when about to give up, your eyes will fall on two or three books at much cheaper prices than elsewhere.

Only last year I spotted a first edition of Harry Plunkett Green's "Where the Bright Waters Meet"—one of the most delightful of all trout fishing books—on a junk stall in a South London market. It was wedged among dog-eared paperbacks and broken-backed detective fiction and cost the princely sum of 15p. The current price for this volume

# SHELF

## *Collecting old fishing books by GERRY HUGHES*

**SPECIALIST ANGLING BOOKSELLERS**

R. J. Coleby,
104 High Street,
Billinghay, Lincoln,
LN4 4ED

Barn Book Supply,
88 Crane Street,
Salisbury, Wilts

E. Chalmers Hallam,
Earlswood,
Egmont Drive,
Avon Castle,
Ringwood, Hants.,
BH24 2BN

Thomas Thorp,
47 Holborn Viaduct,
London, EC1

Anglebooks,
2 Cecil Court,
London, WC2

R. Way,
Brettons,
Burrough Green,
Newmarket, Suffolk

from a specialist dealer is between £15 and £20, so the half-hour visit to the market was well worthwhile.

Another possible source is a local auction room, which deals mainly with household effects. Auctions don't turn up many books but occasionally provide rich pickings. They are generally sold as a boxful and each box needs careful examination on viewing day as the contents are rarely sorted out beforehand. You may discover half-a-dozen fishing books buried under a pile of old novels or a heap of paperbacks. If the books are part of a house clearance, and the house belonged to an angler with a reasonable library, then you have really struck it lucky. They will cost a little more than in a street market because auctions naturally attract dealers who are quick to snap up a possible bargain while waiting for their own particular lots to come up.

The most obvious place to look is in a local bookshop. Not a big shop with clean shelves full of new books hot off the presses but a secondhand bookshop tucked away off the main street. These shops are run by people who know and love books and they will all have a specialist knowledge of some sort. But the one thing many of them have in common is a lack of specialised knowledge about fishing books—which again gives an amateur collector a better chance of picking up a bargain.

In my experience, many back-street booksellers don't even know if they have any fishing books on their shelves. They invariable say "I don't think we have any at the moment." But don't turn away. It's just as likely they have got one or two but they're so involved with their own particular speciality that other subjects just don't register. Browse among the shelves marked Natural History of Sport and you've a good chance of finding something. Failing that, try the Miscellaneous shelf—I've picked up a few useful additions to my library that way.

Bookshop prices will be higher than in other places because a bookseller is in business to make money but if you know your subject you can still buy well. I visited a military history specialist who had two Zane Grey first editions tucked away on his odds and ends shelf—"The Angler's Eldorado" and "Tales of Virgin Seas", both published in the 1920s. They were in almost mint condition and the asking price was £5 each. I snapped up both because I knew (but the bookseller didn't) that either book was worth £25.

There are times in book collecting when you have to back your judgment with hard cash—often more cash than you think you can afford. But if your judgment is right you can be quids in. A bookseller who dealt in a number of different subjects offered me for £35, a first edition of William Scrope's "Days and Nights of Salmon Fishing", published in 1843. At that time I had never heard of Scrope and had never paid anything like that price for a book (nor have I done since).

The bookseller was shrewd enough to know this was a better book than his normal run-of-the mill volumes and I was bold enough to back my judgment with the £30 we eventually settled at. Luckily I was right. When I got home I checked with several collector friends and found the book was worth £90. It's current market value is around £140.

If time is short, save yourself a lot of trouble by buying directly from the half-dozen of so specialist bookdealers who cater for the angler. They are men whose knowledge of the many books written on the subject is deep and detailed and who can supply any book of your choice. Their prices are higher than other sources but what you pay in cash you save in time. Their business is conducted mainly by post and they regularly send out catalogues of all the books in stock, listed alphabetically under an author's name. You can see at a glance what they have and how much it costs. The abbreviations they use tell a great deal about the book itself. A book described as 110pp, cold. ill, dw, ep, teg, means that the book has 110 pages, coloured illustrations, a dust wrapper, endpapers and that the top edge is finished in gilt.

It's so easy to make the mistake of collecting for collecting's sake and end up with a row of books on the shelf. My advice is to search out those authors whose writings give you the greatest pleasure. Of course it will be a purely personal choice but if you are a keen coarse angler you are sure to enjoy anything by J. W. Martin, who wrote under the pen name of "Trent Otter", and whose books were published just after the turn of the century. H. T. Sheringham of the same period is another author for reading time and time again.

If you are a carp fan go for BB's (pen name for Dennis Watkins Pythford) "Confessions of a Carp Fisher" and "A Carp Water"—both now collector's items. Maurice Wiggin wrote some delightful books between 1949 and 1965. Fred J. Taylor and Dick Walker have written thousands of words of good, solid commonsense worthy of a place on anyone's bookshelf and there are many, many more.

More books have been written on fishing than any other sporting subject so it's impossible to list, or even suggest, most of the authors. Most of them cover game fishing in its various forms, with coarse fishing second and sea fishing a poor third.

The most famous fishing book of all time, Izaac Walton's "Compleat Angler" wasn't the first on the subject, nor is a good copy particularly valuable. There have been over 400 different editions since it was first published in 1653. The earliest book on fishing is Dame Juliana Berners "The Treatyse of fysshynge wyth an Angle", published as long ago as 1496. The "Arte of Angling", written by an anonymous author and published in 1577, is thought to be the source of Walton's inspiration for the "Compleat Angler".

Don't bother to look for the rarest book of all. Only one copy of Joseph Crawhall's "Angling Quips and Sporting Skits" was printed back in the last century and it is now in America's Harvard University Library.

Rarities are things that even the most specialised collector can only dream about. But there are still good opportunities to build up a sound library of interesting and entertaining reading. Do make sure that you keep books in good condition. Site the bookshelves so that the books are not exposed to bright sunshine streaming through the window—or the covers will fade. Don't leave them lying about for others to stand cups or glasses on them. And keep them out of reach of small children and their felt-tip pens!

# Collecting old picture postcards
## by SYLVIA MARIE HAYNES

The expert and the novice

**G**ONE fishing? Having a whale of a time? I certainly am— but my angle is collecting picture postcards on humour and I hope you enjoy the Editor's selection of my Victorian and Edwardian angling postcards reproduced in the colour pages of this Annual.

Compared with postal history and stamp collecting, postcards have developed in recent years into one of the most popular collecting hobbies. Not only do postcards cover so many different subjects, they also fascinate from the point of view of various artists and photographers describing and seeing the same subject.

I've spent the last seven years looking for the right cards that will enable me to research and compile my "creative expressions" of visual interest as books to catch the eye . . . all for my dream of a Museum of Cards. I have also found great delight in arranging posters with 12 to 14 cards to each subject for exhibition purposes. And I've compiled a little book on "Fishing Humour", holding many more postcards, trade and cigarette cards and other goodies, as a gift book for anglers.

I hope to hold many exhibitions of postcards and other items in my Museum of Cards as a look-and-learn for children of all ages . . . a visual history aid . . . something of interest to give pleasure to everyone.

But, at the time of writing, the right home for my Museum has still to be found. Hopefully, by the time you read this it will be established— if not in London perhaps at Hay-on-Wye which many anglers will know from their visits to the lovely River Wye.

Maybe I've tempted you to combine your interest in fishing with collecting. So let me tell you a little about the history of postcards and where to buy them.

Humour in fishing has been with us since time immemorial but it is only a little over 100 years ago that postcards were first issued in Austria and then appeared in Britain in the following year 1870. No pictorial matter was seen until 1882 and before March of that year, postcards were used for messages only.

It is believed that the first picture postcard was produced by George Stewart of Edinburgh and F. T. Corket, of Leicester, in 1894, followed rapidly by other firms such as Tucks and Valentines— two of the most prolific and finest publishers in this country.

Messages on the address side of a postcard were not allowed until 1897, so until then all pictorial matter had to allow space for whatever personal message was sent.

The rapid advance in the technique of photographic reproduction enabled postcards to record changing social habits and, subsequently, to interpret tastes in humour and fashion. Then, at the end of the last century, many brilliant illustrators began to design postcards.

If you wish to know more about postcards, try your local library for "The Picture Postcard and Its Origins", by Frank Staff, "Pictures In The Post" by Richard Carline or "Picture Postcards Of The Golden Age" by Toni and Valmai Holt. All these books are out of print but some postcard dealers may have a few for sale.

Which brings me to dealers—and to where to find a good selection of old postcards. Many dealers, from all over England and overseas, advertise in a fine magazine called "Postcard Collectors' Gazette", started and founded by Valerie Monahan and now edited by David Pearlman. The magazine will help you locate postcard auctions, postcard clubs and dealers near to where you live. Dates of Collectors' Fairs are also given—these are great fun and held in most big towns.

There is also "Postcard World", the journal of Postcard Club of Great Britian, formed in 1961 by Mrs Drene Brennan. You can meet her at the "Gazebo", Camden Passage, Angel, Islington, North London, and browse through her large stock of cards.

These days, the price of collecting can spoil the joy of collecting. Price trends have been affected by inflation and a tremendous upsurge of interest in old postcards has also increased values very quickly. There are two price catalogues—"I.P.M." and "Picton's".

●A two-page display of some angling postcards from Mrs Haynes' collection will be found on pages 62 and 63.

The throat teeth in a 3 lb. chub can crush a finger almost to pulp, says John Wilson. That's how he learned—the hard way!—to seek winter chub with small livebaits.

# CHUB VEBAIT

## by John Wilson

The first time I saw a chub taken on livebait was many years ago during a morning's piking on the Great Ouse at Godmanchester and the event was quite a shock. It was inconceivable to me then that a mere 1¾ lb. chub could grab and actually swallow a six-inch roach complete with snap tackle and I mistakenly treated the catch as a fluke.

But several years later I found out what a chub's throat teeth are really like when a 3 lb. fish crunched my right forefinger almost to pulp as I tried to poke a hook clear of its throat. This really sent me after chub with a vertgeance and I very soon realised their liking for a small livebait and their astonishing ability to consume it—fast!

These days I carry a pair of pharyngeal teeth with me as a keepsake and conversation piece, but I've never regretted learning the hard way and I often fancy a roving livebaiting session after chub in preference to a sit-out routine—particularly in cold or really foul weather when concentration is hard to maintain.

My tackle differs little from a summer freelining outfit of 11 foot Avon rod, 5 lb. line and size 6 or 4 eyed hook, tied direct. The exception is a tiny ⅝ in. pilot float plugged to the line by an inch of peacock quill, which I set to fish the bait six inches shallower than the swim. I pinch on a swan shot around 18 inches from the hook to take the bait down, and grease the line for about 30 yards so that I can trot down long glides or alongside trailing alder branches without any unnatural dragging. This is a most important point.

Baits are invariably 2-3 inch dace, gudgeon or roach. Minnows are quite deadly but seem to do a disappearing act from my local stretches of the Wensum during the winter and I often wish I could obtain some bleak (a rarity in Norfolk waters).

Bleak are the chub livebait supreme on most of the larger southern rivers, but almost any small fish will suffice so long as it is silvery and lively. If the bait is presented properly (hooked through the top lip) a chub will generally oblige by walloping it up almost as soon as it starts to trot down.

There is nothing to stop pike nobbling small livebaits and if the chub are wary pike can be a real nuisance, especially when a "double" takes hold and bites through the line just as you are about to feel confident of beating the odds!

One way to minimise the number of "jacks" is to search only those chub swims which produced fish earlier in the year. My favourites are where alder or willow trees hang well out over the water. They seldom fail to produce chub, which feel safe beneath their branches and find extra shelter from danger or heavy floodwater by hiding in the holes carved out beneath the tree roots.

A long glide bordered by half-a-dozen alders could easily support 30 or more chub and providing they are not spooked by clumsy casting or bankside vibrations it is sometimes possible to take a brace or three in a very short spell before moving on.

At times you may fish several swims before getting a take and when the pilot float does finally zoom under, it is so easy to deliberate and wait before striking, as in pike fishing. But don't. Hit any sort of take immediately and as hard as you dare.

A chub doesn't grab a bait like pike. It engulfs it in that huge mouth and sucks it back to those powerful throat teeth for mincing. So if you hesitate, they will feel the float and cough up the bait. Or, you may very well get back only the head of the bait and that's a sure sign of a chub run.

Maximum mobility is most important when roving for chub, so keep tackle requirements to an absolute minimum. One rod, landing net and bait bucket are quite enough to manage when sleuthing along through bankside vegetation—much of which does not entirely die off in the winter, especially brambles. As always, small items such as hooks, floats, shot, forceps and so on are permanent residents of my battered fishing jacket.

But if a camera does not add to your burden, take one along. A real specimen is always on the cards when fishing with livebaits.

Newcomers to freshwater fishing sometimes land in trouble because they think the fishing is free if they don't have to buy a day or period ticket. The riparian owner of any water—lake, pond, river or canal—may allow free fishing but a rod licence is needed from the Water Authority controlling the area in which the water is situated.

Ten regional authorities cover everything to do with water in England and Wales and each issues its own fishing licence.

Like a driving licence, which gives official permission to drive but without supplying a vehicle, a water authority licence gives the right to use a rod on the waters in its area but without giving permission to fish in private waters.

# ARE YOU LICENSED?

So a licence is needed before fishing, PLUS the owner's permission in club or privately controlled waters.

Licences are usually available in local tackle shops but if in any difficulty, write to the address of the appropriate authority on the list.

Remember, fishing without a rod licence can mean ending up in court. They don't have detector vans but they do have burly bailiffs!

GERRY HUGHES

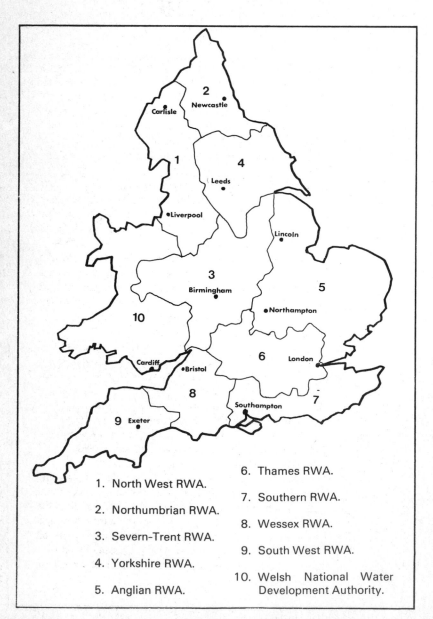

1. North West RWA.

2. Northumbrian RWA.

3. Severn-Trent RWA.

4. Yorkshire RWA.

5. Anglian RWA.

6. Thames RWA.

7. Southern RWA.

8. Wessex RWA.

9. South West RWA.

10. Welsh National Water Development Authority.

## WATER AUTHORITIES

ANGLIAN WATER AUTHORITY, Diploma House, Grammar School Walk, Huntingdon PE18 6NZ.

NORTHUMBRIAN WATER AUTHORITY, Northumbria House, Regent Centre, Gosforth, Newcastle upon Tyne NE3 3PX.

NORTH WEST WATER AUTHORITY, Dawson House, Great Sankey, Warrington WA5 3LW.

SEVERN-TRENT WATER AUTHORITY, Abelson House, Coventry Road, Sheldon, Birmingham B26 3PU.

SOUTHERN WATER AUTHORITY, Guildbourne House, Worthing, Sussex BN11 1LD.

SOUTH WEST WATER AUTHORITY, 3–5 Barnfield Road, Exeter EX1 1RE.

THAMES WATER AUTHORITY, New River Head, Rosebery Avenue, London EC1R 4TP.

WELSH NATIONAL WATER DEVELOPMENT AUTHORITY, Cambrian Way, Brecon, Powys LD3 7HP.

WESSEX WATER AUTHORITY, Techno House, Redcliffe Way, Bristol BS1 6NY.

YORKSHIRE WATER AUTHORITY, West Riding House, 67 Albion Street, Leeds LS1 5AA.

# Falling Leaves

## By TOM WILLIAMS

Poachers, pollution and predators pose formidable problems in the life of a riverkeeper who stands guard over miles of valuable fishing. The successful 'keeper is firm but good-humoured with the first, watchful for signs of the second and usually well-armed to deal with the third.

These problems may sound dramatic to a "townie" but a countryman takes them in his stride.

As Fishery Manager of a big country estate in the Hampshire Avon valley, Tom Williams copes with it all, plus the technical and commercial supervision of a rapidly expanding trout farm that has developed in a few years from a hole in the ground to one of the biggest enterprises in the freshwater farming industry.

Very few of the thousands of readers of Angler's Mail have ever met Tom but they follow the highlights of his life every week through his popular "My River" column.

Each year, Angler's Mail Annual reprints a carefully chosen selection of Tom's earlier notes and records them in this more permanent form.

## *Fantasy world in a willow jungle*

I WONDER if we fishermen ever grow up, or are we children to the end of our days? Upstream from this cottage, where the angler follows the main river through bends and across the shallows, there are areas of low-lying ground that have become near-derelict water meadows. A nature reserve that harbours the occasional lonely otter through the summer and the wandering bittern in the cold part of the year.

It is one of those places where any tree that falls is left to gather a canopy of bramble, interwoven with old man's beard and the saplings of another year's growth. The effect is a series of Indian tents, the most secret place in all the world for youngsters.

In some sort of wish to get away, I pushed along a carrier bank and was met by a dog that looked as near like a fox as colour and shape would allow it, but legs that belonged to the collie family lifted it well clear of the ground and called it a dog. There would have been doubt in my mind had I had a twelve-bore with me.

In the midst of a willow jungle there was a camp that wouldn't have been out of place somewhere along the Amazon, or maybe north of Nigeria. There was a tree house, a battered boat and out from the bank stuck a couple of rods that lacked nothing of the modern angler. Into this world of childish fantasy, smoke from a fire gave a fog of unreality. Small faces peering from among trees, left me with a feeling of having walked somewhere where I was most certainly not welcome.

They were trespassing against the fishing and the security of the Estate and yet, with their catch of dace and small roach, were obviously planning a self-sufficient life that intruded into nobody's privacy. We hardly passed a word, except that their russet-coloured hound defended valiantly against my two alsatians, possessing the advantage of the home ground, plus the support of the crowd (three small boys).

Later that day as I sat at home, Scotch in hand, log fire stoked up the chimney, I watched a TV programme from Cumberland. A gentleman living in that part of the world, well-known for his writings and television programmes, set out to show us his life along the Eskdale valley where I had spent part of my youth.

Then suddenly it clicked, the reason why the lump in the throat for those youngsters on the back carrier was rekindled by Hugh Falkus fishing the Esk at night. There is the same sort of secretive life buried below the skin of all of us, for there was no difference in that life along the Cumberland rivers with a senior member of the community than that of those grubby-nosed kids.

Pedigree labradors and mongrels, Daisy air rifle and Purdy shot gun, 4 lb. sea trout instead of dace and a modernised farm-house likened unto that rough tent among the trees. Age is in the heart, not in the legs.

# Rats for the mink

**W**ITH the harvest in, rats that would have moved to the old-fashioned corn stack now find it difficult to gain access to grain driers. They look for easier pickings and descend on the trout farm. Autumn-cleaned banks become marked with fresh burrows and squealing rodents chase each other across our access paths. When the floodlights come on at nights they view them as a second moon and carry on their nocturnal habits in the full glare.

In accepting the trout farm as an alternative to the security of the cornfields they make a mistake, for our resident population of wild mink quickly seize on this additional diet.

We watched a small black bitch mink work through rat burrows with all the expertise of a ferret in a rabbit warren. Rats fleeing before her and being shot while she, not nervous of the noise, hunted on. In this busy period of the farm we have picked up two of these resident hunters and are bewitched by their apparent tameness and the good they do us.

# Autumn migrants

**W**E had an osprey stay a day or so in its autumn passage south, a grey bird of considerable size when lifting off the branch of a dead tree to take its long glide over the soft clean waters of the Avon. It stayed on the lower end of the fish farm and moved on during the night.

It seems we are in the flight path of their southerly migration, which is a non-hurried affair, but not the flight path of the nesting route which must be more hurried, like the migration of a salmon to spawn once the eggs are near ripe.

I saw a hen harrier in the most unusual place of halfway across the Channel midway between Le Havre and Southampton. It did its slow flight of flap, flap, flap and glide across the ups and downs of mid-Channel breakers, heading for the Dordogne Valley which I had just left.

A single swallow zig-zagged past the ship and a cluster of martins landed on the rails of the upper deck. For an hour or so they travelled in the wrong direction until their tired bodies lifted off and headed south.

# Another import problem—this time it's weed

**G**AMEKEEPERS and riverkeepers often talk of import problems. We do not mean the balance of trade but the grey squirrel, the increasing numbers of collared dove that have exported themselves from Scandinavia and my own problems of imported mink and weed along the valley.

We have six lakes that mysteriously filled with Canadian weed, the same weed that blocks the 200 screens on trout farm and other streams, a weed that grows to a given length below the surface and jibs at breaking through into absolute light.

Imported years ago for aquarium enthusiasts it now transports its seed pods into every nook and cranny of these Isles. Even on the chalk streams, each slack corner where the mud holds contains a piece.

Now we have another pest. A carrier stream where the only flow is used through fish holding tanks suddenly blocks. The culprit is a strange fernlike weed that has overlaid the duck weed and grown into a thick blanket like some strange vegetable animal cross from another world.

It makes the surface look like a smooth lawn and has deceived more than one dog which tried to walk on it. This weed, the Azolla or Water Fairy Fern, started clogging the surface of some of the slower flowing carriers, roofing over the stream bed so that everything died beneath it. Where there is no light there is very little life. Azolla was imported for the aquarium tank and is rapidly building up to be a worse nuisance than Canadian weed.

# The restless eels

**I**F there is one time in the year that tinges a riverkeeper's life with excitement it's the moment when the leaves take a turn in colour and the sun gets lower in the southern sky. Trees and grasses start to lose their growth and every small shower of rain puts a touch of colour into the river.

A running-off of water from the plough, a laying of dust and a thousand small riverside drains stain with brown from the soil instead of running clear. In this darkened water atmosphere the eel begins its restless move down to the sea.

During the weed cut a few weeks ago one of the operators saw an eel sunning itself on the shallows. It was, according to him, of unbelievable size. He prophesied that if this particular eel was caught on its seaward migration it would create some sort of a record in the eel trap. He talked of the riverkeeper being backed into a corner and of the menace from those dark round sea-going eyes. That's all as maybe but it would be nice to believe the exaggeration involved.

We have started eeling, cleaning the rocks and taking half-a-dozen eels per night, ranging from 1 lb. to 4 lb. with several of the larger fish showing scars of some unfortunate fisherman's loss.

While this smattering of eels migrate on rising water, there has been a corresponding push of autumn salmon going upstream. A sudden opening of hatches to let autumn rubbish through has become a crack in the door for our captive salmon. It shows what these travelling fish will do providing there is a hole for them to follow.

# Reading the riot act

I MET three young lads from the village school sitting on the river bank where the chalk stream bends through a mill pool, where the water is clear and a hundred trout feed on the shrimp washed over the weir crest.

*There is only one way for a good fishery manager to explore the bed of a lake—get in and do it the hard way as personally demonstrated by Tom Williams!*

They smiled and knew in their non-fishing approach to the water that I would leave them and be thankful they were up to no more mischief than envy of the mill pool fish.

It would have been all right had they killed the fish before slipping them into the lining of their jackets, for even as I stood, beaming down, the twisting of the live fish flipped their jackets this way and that.

Hand lines dropped into the depths of the mill pool as I approached were abandoned and like a partridge covey, they flushed in all directions with trout and dace being dropped on the road as they ran. We collared them and took them home to their mums, read the riot act to smiling parents and gave them the fish as a happy bonus.

# New recruits on the bank

WHEN Spring blood creeps into young anglers' veins they apply to be riverkeepers. They sink their thoughts into shoals of letters, plead their wishes in a summer flood and because we are expanding we are persuaded. But is it riverkeeper they want to be or park keeper with a peaked hat and a mobile recording of "Have you got a permit, sir?"

Their idea of the life is to walk it with fishing rod in hand and not to work with fish. Not all of them—something like 30 per cent. The sort of youngster that fits the scene is a young village lad from just down the way, never a keen angler in his youth, more a potterer around.

A short stick from the hedge, a length of line with hooks and any natural bait that falls available. A dropper-in of snails into hatch pools, an instant poacher without the instant method.

**London anglers Barry and Norman Brock with two big barbel caught from Tom Williams' stretch of the Hampshire Avon. Barry's fish (left) weighed 12½ lb and Norman's tipped the scales at 11 lb.**

Edward has been with me for near 12 months, spends his days pottering around the countryside, has become a skilled bridge builder and for some silly reason, enjoys walking behind a grass cutting machine, finding satisfaction in the deed.

He has a companion now, in fact two companions. One is a blonde-haired lad who has joined him on the river from the local school, a lad who worked his apprenticeship after school hours and during the holidays, proved his ability to get on with anglers and to work alone before we took him on.

The other companion in this Huckleberry Finn life is a non-English speaking Spaniard, a student from Spain whose father runs a fishery in the hills above Bilbao and

visits us to see our ways both with anglers and fish farm.

This young bronzed lad from the Bay of Biscay, with handsome Latin appearance, is learning English mixed with fishing terms of groundbait and long-trotting and how he is going to use that back in Spain.

This high mink-breeding year, with mortality among the litters almost nil, has given these youngsters a summer evening's pastime of finding holts among the rushes, sharp-shooting to the head of the black fellows as they lift cunningly on the edge of the passing river. A competition for pelts, the gamekeeper's gibbet festooned with strange immigrant shapes.

They know these pelts have a value near a week's wage come the autumn. They know that with every summer mink that dies, they lose a Christmas bonus. Yet still they continue the barrage.

# Fishing by committee

IT rained in the week, the sort of rain that our farmers give thanks for, a gentle drizzle that increases so slowly that you are wet to the skin without realising the intensity of the fall, a warm wetness that is no way uncomfortable.

It leaves the corn standing and puts a green mist over the hard-baked earth, sets flies a-buzzing and the flowers to open in a renewed burst of summer colour.

It does nothing for the river that still runs clear, way below the high water marks on the leaning willow, doesn't disturb the gathered rubbish in the river bays and leaves undisturbed the holted chub that lurks in the shadow of that same rubbish.

We leaned on trees, watched the barbel show and sent a fisherman out across the wadable water to stand at a point upstream. Then we directed him from afar, with instructions of up a bit, down a bit, so that we who gathered on the bank were doing the fishing while he in the water did the work.

The committee changed bait discussion, sent the message out to midstream and moved to bread, worm, maggot, to bait-dropper hung in the midst of the shoal. A couple of trout, a small chub of maybe two pounds and our fisherman in midstream looked askance for more instructions, while another meeting decided to send one of their number to search for crayfish.

Eventually, we hooked a smallish barbel of maybe five or six pounds that weaved its way in and out of the willow roots and in its speed did away with all this committee work and a need of a chairman to do the representing.

We all shouted together, pull this way, lift its head, keep him out of the trees, 'til poor Barry in the centre of the river didn't know whether he was coming or going. It was Barry who lost the fish was the general opinion, though the same committee's opinion varied on the size from near-record to the complete reverse.

# On training dogs

I'VE trained dogs to be dogs to all people, to be companions to retrieve fish and fowl. And I've taught my latest batch of Alsatians to chase the birds from the trout stews, to keep the seagulls on the move and do it with a sense of enjoyment. I've even tried with "Spinner", my own dog, to get him into some sort of retrieving mind, to be a dual purpose dog, to be a gun dog as well as a bird dog.

"Spinner" resisted all attempts to teach him to retrieve fish and his bird chasing has been reduced to wagtails, for which he has developed an intense delight. Thank God he isn't gun shy. The reverse, perhaps, for he shakes the carbide banger, accepts the cannon boom into his face, drags it to the water and drowns it.

Now at last his mind is beginning to work. He has realised the importance of what I am trying to tell him. As soon as I put the 12-bore to the shoulder he is all attention, the moment of his duty is at hand.

I fire at some miserable seagull and watch it waft into the next county, break the gun, eject the cartridge and "Spinner" retrieves the empty cases. Surely that's what I've been trying to teach him, he says.

I stuff another eel in his mouth and say "Fetch it".

# A fresh look at old barriers

WHEN those old-timers in the sixteenth century laid down the water meadows they thought, I am sure, they were providing an early bite of grass for sheep and little else. It meant more stock carried through the winter, surviving as warmer-than-atmosphere warmed the roots of meadow grass.

Water was impounded for mills, each mill being the centre of five or six homes and a family's living depending on such small occupations as hatch or weedrack cleaning, or, as one old friend of mine now in his nineties says: "Owning the horse that helped loaded waggons out of the valley meant a 5 a.m. start and a midnight finish!"

There were fish, as a right, from the surroundings of the mill and eels as a Royal dish from the built-in trap.

Those water-controlled hatches, ancient and modern, are now under the microscope of officialdom. They are being examined from every angle, from flood control

**A Hampshire Avon weirpool in low summer conditions . . .**

through to obstruction to migrating fish.

They are the cause of so much friction up and down our chalk stream that backs are turned on friends, accusations levelled and dark deeds committed in the night hours. Metal water stops are taken out and wooden hatches shut when they must stay open. The value of running salmon is equated against the friendship of just about everyone.

Years ago, when I keepered the Itchen, the salmon shooting season opened in December, when broad backs stood out of water on shallow redds. Keepers shot them and added their carcasses to the rosebush fertiliser.

A wire noose and a loaded set of trebles made sure that salmon were kept where they belonged in the lower stretches of the chalk stream.

Those ancient water meadow makers were the fathers of the method that still keep our South country salmon down there near the sea.

To salmon entering the River Wye system, 60 miles is a gentle cruise upstream for a Spring fish and sealice that dislike freshwater still live at Hereford.

How different our Southern fish; on Test, Itchen and Avon they meet a barrier of hatches just above the tide line and according to the river flow have to choose a route that could lead into some impassable corner, a metal hatch with a six-foot head and a water velocity in its underflow exceeding the speed that a salmon can swim.

# Summer and salmon arrive

SUDDENLY, summer has overwhelmed a Spring that got off on the wrong foot. Days were cold, the wind came out of the east, and a soft winter that didn't mellow got colder and pushed blossoms off the trees, killed pear and plum, did no good at all to the apple.

April's showers came in a couple of days, warmed the river with extra water to the mid-fifties, sprouted the blackthorn, took the bare hawthorn through to green in a matter of hours. So summer was here in April, and it was deckchairs and open-neck shirts instead of pullovers, waterproofs and a warm car.

Salmon smolts running the water meadow arrived in droves at the trout screens and were lifted over and sent on with good wishes for a safe journey. How many millions died in water meadows, suffocated trying to run the Spring push of grass?

The scent of early summer has changed these years. Once it was the sweet of fresh-cut hay, the sickly-sour smell of cattle grazing that came across the river in an eddying breeze. Now its silage, and the chemical that kills both insects and supposed weed, lies in the air in a sickly smell, the tractor driver masked against the risk.

Spring or summer nevertheless, I caught my first salmon in the week, lost one and dragged another from the water. I had an abortive morning with fishermen around my ears and we sat and yarned and hung a Devon from the Trafalgar hatches. With too light a lead the spinning Devon showed in the white water, a place where no fish of commonsense would pause to take a bait.

We hung in melancholy groups, finally retreating from a fishless morning, they en route to "The Bull" while I paced the river bank back home. A fresh fish head and tailed as I passed, gave the traditional sign of "Here-I-am, come-and-get-me". A small two-inch yellow Devon drifted across that fish's vision, its fluttering flight encouraging her to remember the feed of yesterday.

Once hooked, the salmon ran downstream to a slack pool, a point of land where the water loses all sense of direction clean earth on the far side, vegetation growing out under my feet. It boiled across the river as if to run ashore, turned and made the gathering of slack line urgent, then came in and delved into the roots of the overhanging canopy beneath me. It fought as fish can do when their life is at risk, and died as they must if they make THE mistake.

The lost fish was one of those that will grace the redds this coming Autumn. It took the bait and paused to think, hung on the end of the line vibrating through to the butt. Then it felt the pull that gave it the direction of its flight, turned and ran through the hatches to the lower water and went on to the sea 30 miles away. The hooks pulled out and another fishy memory was added to fish unseen, of uncertain size that will grow with the telling.

I caught a 20-pounder later the same day, or rather shared it with another angler. I hooked it, he did the fighting and we shared the pleasures but not the fish. At £2 a pound it is as if we were fishing for gold.

Those hatches where I lost my fish are a trap to the inexperienced. You tighten too hard and the sheer weight of water washes the fish into the lower level. Then, if you are not strong enough in the walking up the fish fights and makes it there in his own right.

Yesterday, Nobby, well aware that nobody has landed a fish of more than 25 lb. in this position, hooked a 27-pounder, killed its first run across the hatches and apparently landed it without effort, and now he smugly tells the tale.

How pretty that fish was! The silver bloom, the weight hidden in the shoulder, hidden so that I bet him a pound its weight was $24\frac{1}{2}$ lb., while he and his non-knowledgeable friends stuck to a 27 lb. guess that was based on nothing more than a wish.

I lost my quid to their expertise. This sadly out of line guessing of weights has continued. Where once I was within an ounce I am pounds out this year. The width across the shoulder seems to have increased, the amount of feed they have taken from the sea improved.

**. and the same weirpool in late Autumn when the rains came.**

**Netting operations in progress on one of the lakes controlled by Tom.**

# 'Grandpa' barbel causes a stir

**B**ARBEL have always interested me and because of this I have played around with them in all sorts of ways, mainly because I know that the record could be broken by a weight margin that would make it worthwhile . . . and I am thinking now of a particular fish that must be all of 20 lb.

In the past few years I have moved barbel from Kennet to Avon and Upper Thames and Avon to Stour. I once ran a hatchery with limited success, where a million odd barbel eggs were nursed to putrefaction.

I had a captive fish for five years, put it in a stew with large rainbows when it weighed 11 lb. and took it out dead at the end of that time. Despite the abundance of feed on the bottom of the stew its weight had been reduced by a couple of pounds or so. Perhaps the competition for the sinking pellet was too great for it.

I moved seven smallish barbel to the Dorset Allen and put them into the head waters, but in a drought lost them in the upper reaches of the Winterbourne. We have a weir pool fish that shows itself now and again and was once hooked and lost by a salmon angler. We laid siege to it in

the clear water of a hatch pool when the current was diverted a different way.

Then, last week, all our old barbel-keeping interests were revived, for as the minnows shoaled on the shallows at Stanlynch, chub came out from under the roots to feed on the eggs and exhausted fish, and were joined by a shoal of barbel with the granddaddy of them all bringing up the rear.

Here was a fish that would disturb your mind, that laughed at the light tackle necessary to deceive him and would ignore the braided line of heavier offensives.

There is a growing patch of bare earth around the base of the willows where leaning anglers, forsaking all others, desert the salmon rod and fly for trout and wait for this one fish to move. There are "Oh's" and "Ah's", and the mapping out of an opening day campaign that covers the siting of stools, even a wade through deeper water should they hook him.

I feel sorry for them because come opening day the barbel will have got this spawning madness out of his mind and removed himself to a secret holt in the green weed banks of the lower river, perhaps to fall victim to some non-thinker of barbel.

My own idea is that he will show smaller friends the spawning minnows and delight the off-season anglers with his size.